Copyright © 2020 by Keisuke Andrew
All rights reserved. This book or any portion thereof
may not be reproduced or used in any manner whatsoever
without the express written permission of the author
except for the use of brief quotations in a book review.

The information in this book is meant to supplement, not replace, proper martial arts training. Like any sport, martial arts involving speed, equipment, balance and environmental factors poses some inherent risk. The author advises readers to take full responsibility for their safety and know their limits. Before practicing the skills described in this book, be sure that you do not take risks beyond your level of experience, aptitude, training and comfort level. Only practice under the strict supervision of a qualified instructor.

Foreward

My inspiration to write this book was all the new beginner students that walk through the door of my Jiu Jitsu school with similar questions that are a variation of the following. What etiquette or rules do I follow? How do I tie my belt? How often should I come to practice? What are these positions? What are my goals when I roll/spar? I love sharing Jiu Jitsu with everyone and I thought that if there was a book that is simple, easy to read and understand, it might be helpful for all the new Jiu Jitsu students.

I purposefully left all guard passes, sweeps, many concepts and submissions out as I wanted this book to be a guide on your Jiu Jitsu journey, not a book that teaches you all the basic Jiu Jitsu techniques. When you first learn Jiu Jitsu, you will most likely learn that you need to learn positions, then transitions such as sweeps, back takes, then setting up your attack positions and finally submission comes at the very end. I should have left out submissions completely but I felt that they are the most exciting part of Jiu Jitsu so I couldn't help myself.

All the information in this book is just my perspective and outlook as a Jiu Jitsu practitioner and instructor. If there is anything contradicting with the teachings of your Professor, please note that there are many perspectives in Jiu Jitsu and you should always defer to the Instructor that you are under the guidance of in your academy.

Thank you for taking the time to pick up this book. I hope it will help guide you in your Jiu Jitsu journey. If you could rate and/or review this book I would greatly appreciate it! If you are ever in Oregon City, Oregon, I would love for you to come visit Enso Jiu Jitsu!

Keisuke Andrew

About the Author

Keisuke started training Brazilian Jiu Jitsu and Mixed martial arts in 2001 and received his Black belt in 2009. In MMA competition, Keisuke has amassed a record of 5-0 in amateur competition and 3-0 as a pro. Keisuke is the head Instructor of Enso Jiu Jitsu, his own Brazilian Jiu Jitsu Academy in Oregon City, Oregon.

TABLE OF CONTENTS

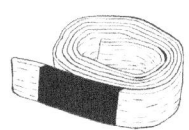

- ORIGIN OF JIU JITSU
- DOJO/ACADEMY ETIQUETTE
- HOW TO TIE YOUR BELT
- SPORTS JIU JITSU ROLL DIAGRAM
- JIU JITSU IN A ONE ON ONE FIGHT
- HIERARCHY OF POSITIONS
- POSITIONS
- SUBMISSIONS
- HOW TO BUILD YOUR GAME

OSOTOGARI (MAJOR OUTER REAP)!

This Samurai is attempting a modified Osotogari. Instead of the collar grip in his left hand, he is pushing his opponent down with his forearm to the throat. Instead of a sleeve grip in his right hand, his is pushing him down with his broken katana!

DOJO/ACADEMY ETIQUETTE

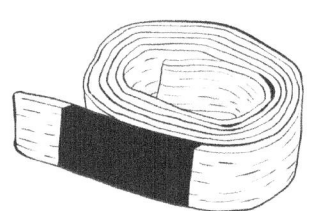

DOJO/ACADEMY ETIQUETTE

Etiquette in this book may or may not apply to your academy so you will want to check with your professor on any uncertain area. Most of these are pretty standard in most academies so if you follow them, you will most likely be fine.

- If you have any contagious illness or skin infection, refrain from training. Even if you think you can get through class, for the sake of everyone you train with, take time off, get better and come back. It is very important that we do everything we can to keep our training partners safe.

- Refer to the black belt instructors as professors, all colored belt instructors as coaches.

- Always be respectful to everyone.

- Never lose your temper. Exercise self-control at all times, this is very important for everyone's safety and your own.

- Refrain from using foul language or profanity. Think of your academy as the place that you are at your best.

- All jewelry, piercings and other items should be removed during training.

- Keep your fingernails and toenails trimmed.

- Training gear and gi should always be kept clean. Wash your gi after every training session.

- Avoid wearing garments showing inappropriate wording or images.

- No shoes on the mat.

- If you want to take a photo or video of class, ask the professor and your training partners first.

- If you are late for class, wait outside the mat and ask the instructor for permission to join the class.

HOW TO TIE YOUR BELT

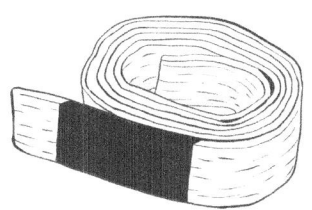

HOW TO TIE YOUR BELT

Beginner's Jiu Jitsu Guide

Hold the belt in your right hand.

Tag on the belt should be on top.

Use your right forearm to lock in your gi.

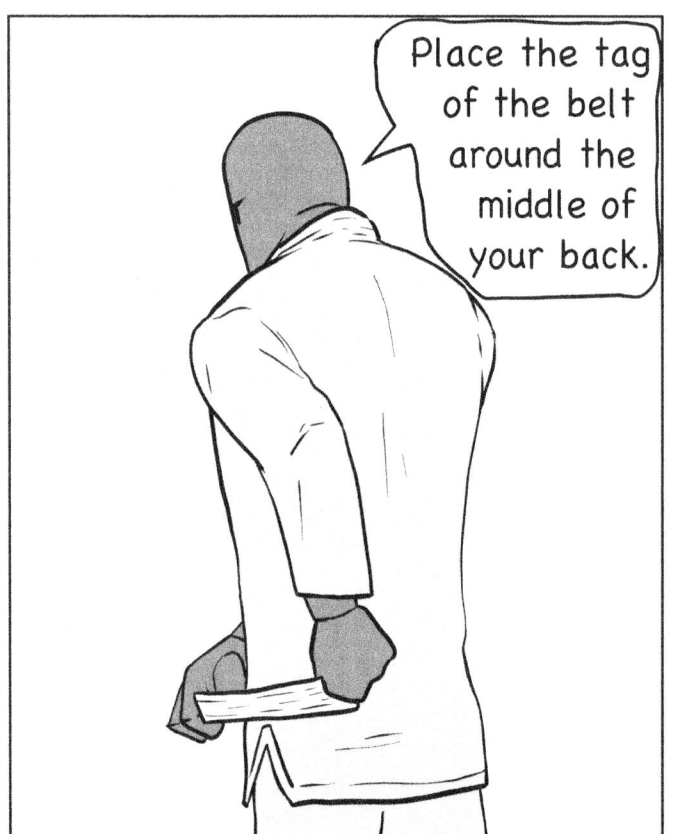

Place the tag of the belt around the middle of your back.

Wrap the belt around your waist two times.

HOW TO TIE YOUR BELT

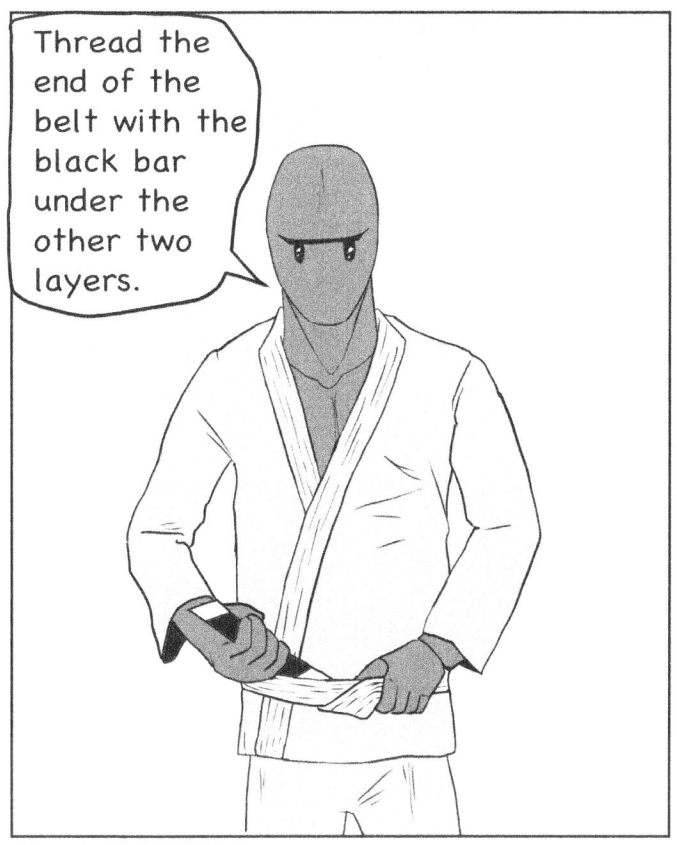

HOW TO TIE YOUR BELT

SPORT JIU JITSU ROLL DIAGRAM

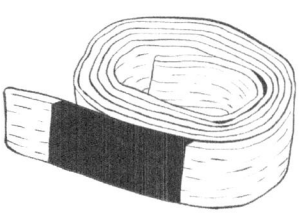

This is a very basic diagram of transitions that take place in a roll. The competitor on top can look for submissions such as leg locks, rolling guillotine and rolling armbar or look to break down their opponent's guard, pass, establish position and then look for submissions. Compared to the competitor on the top, the competitor on the bottom has significantly more submissions at their arsenal. If you are able to get a sweep on your opponent, you typically get to bypass their guard and go immediately into a strong attacking position.

JIU JITSU IN A ONE ON ONE FIGHT

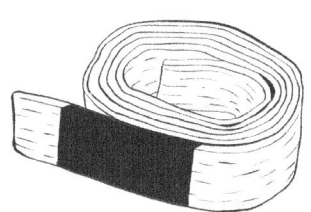

JIU JITSU IN A ONE ON ONE FIGHT

In a fight, you have to minimize your opponent's chance of hurting you and give yourself the best chance of ending the fight. The biggest hurdle is closing the gap between you and your opponent where they have the best chance of landing a strike and taking them down.

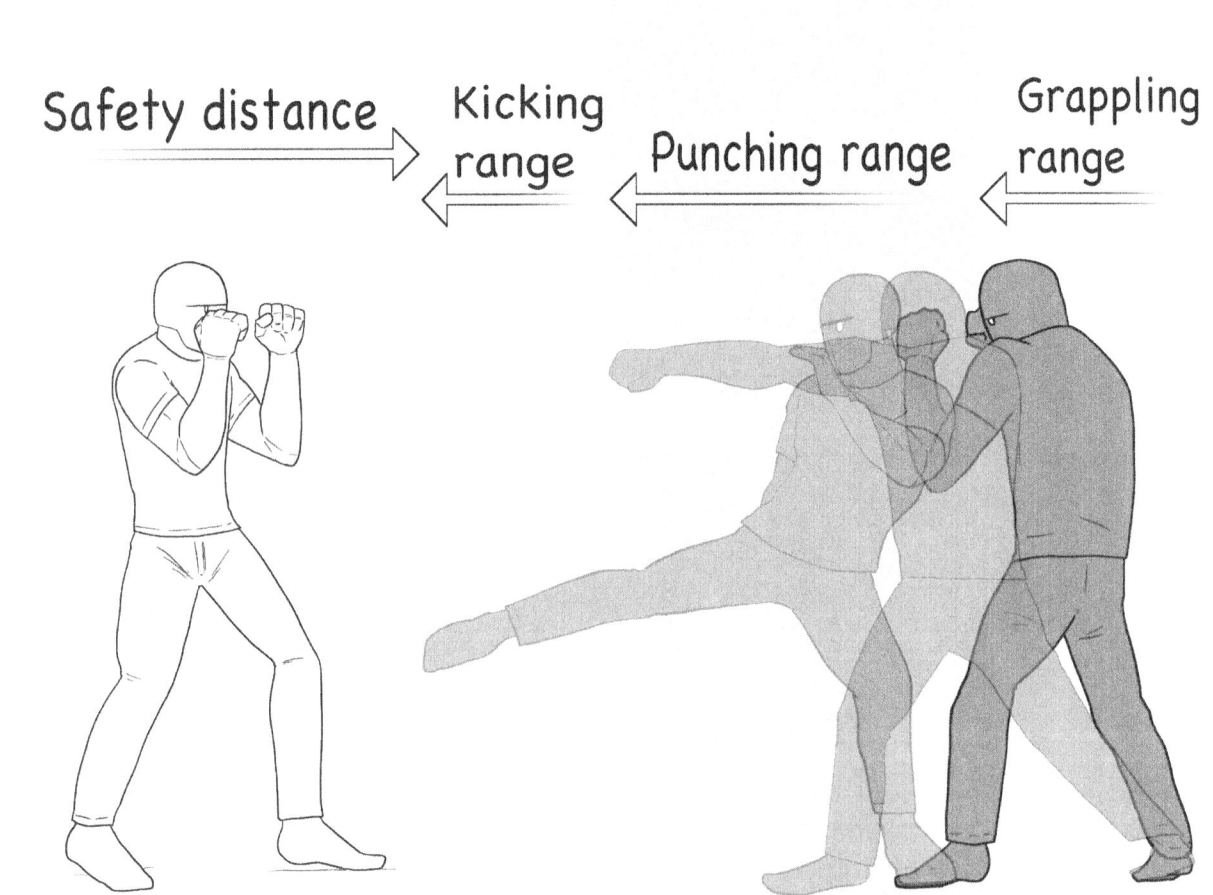

Between the punching range and grappling range is also the range where you can get kneed, elbowed or taken down yourself. Until you are 100% ready to commit to closing in on your opponent, you have to maintain your safety distance with your footwork and strikes of your own.

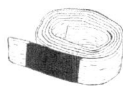 JIU JITSU IN A ONE ON ONE FIGHT

Throwing punches without gloves can be devastating to your hand but, just by threatening your opponent by putting your jabs out will help keep your opponent away and will make it significantly easier to get into your grappling range.

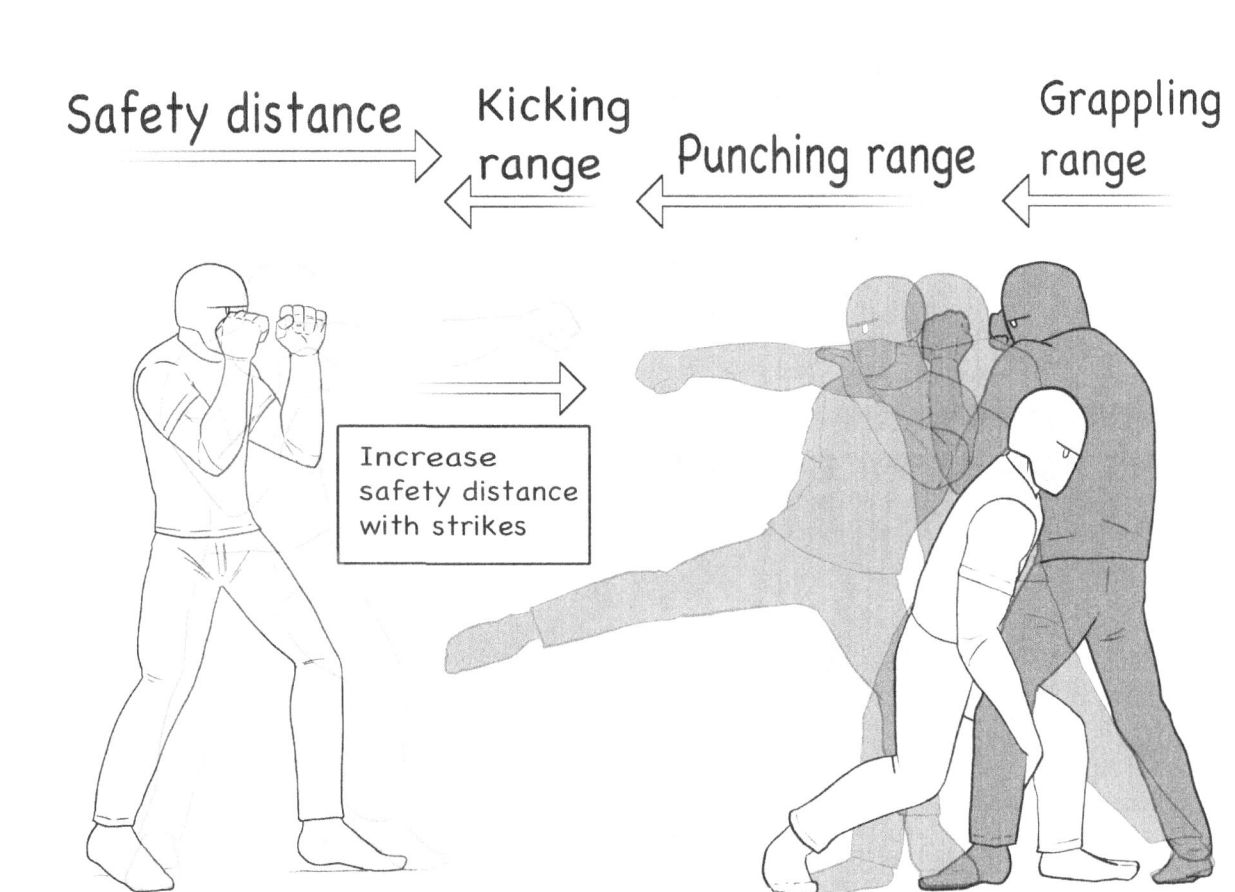

Pay close attention to how your opponent throws strikes, how they move and how they react when you fake a jab or fake a takedown. This will give you valuable information about your opponent's tendencies and when it is safe to close the gap.

JIU JITSU IN A ONE ON ONE FIGHT

FIGHT STANCE

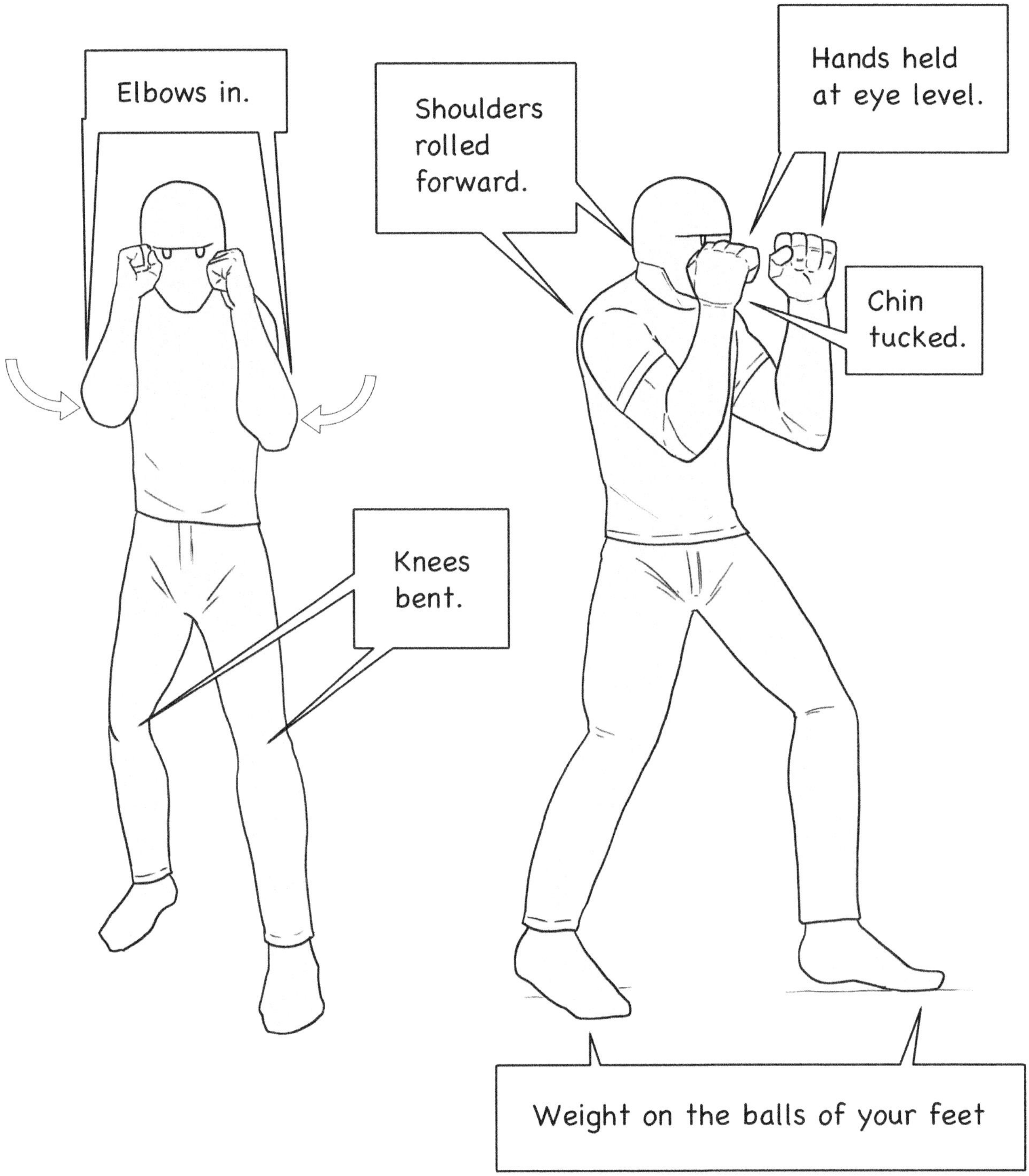

Elbows in.

Shoulders rolled forward.

Hands held at eye level.

Chin tucked.

Knees bent.

Weight on the balls of your feet

HIERARCHY OF POSITIONS

This list is based on Jiu Jitsu as a whole. There are many instances where strikes are mentioned in these position. **You can not hit your opponent in sports Jiu Jitsu.**

Also, this list is not in anyway a official list. This list is the authors perspective from his experience in Jiu Jitsu.

1. **BACK MOUNT**
2. **MOUNT**
3. **KNEE RIDE**
4. **CROSS SIDE**
5. **NORTH SOUTH**
6. **TURTLE TOP**
7. **HALF GUARD TOP**
8. **GUARD TOP**
9. **GUARD BOTTOM**
10. **HALF GUARD BOTTOM**

#1 Back mount: King of all positions, especially if you get your opponent belly down and flattened. When your opponent is turned away from you, they barely have any offense available.

Submissions from position:

Rear naked choke
Armbar
Sliding lapel choke

Transitional position:

Mount (#2): Only transition to mount if you are going to lose back mount.

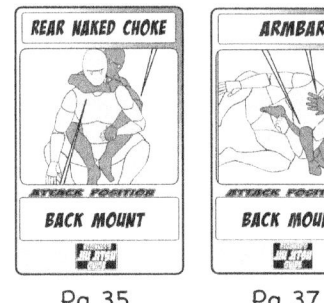
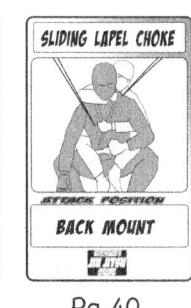

Pg 35   Pg 37   Pg 40

#2 Mount top: This position is 2nd on the list due to the fact that in a fight, you can finish your opponent with strikes or if they turn over, we get the #1 position on this list and finish with a choke.

Submissions from mount:

Cross choke
Armbar
Americana

Transitional positions:

Take back mount (#1) if it becomes available. If you are going to lose mount, switch to knee ride (#3) or go from knee ride to cross side (#4).

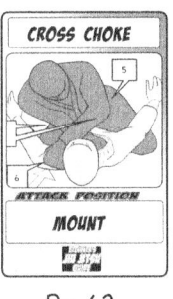

Pg 42   Pg 44   Pg 46

#3 Knee ride top: This is a very difficult position to maintain and attempt submissions from during the beginning stage of your Jiu Jitsu but it's #3 for the fact that in a fight this position is devastating to your opponent as you can land fight-ending strikes or transition easily to mount or cross side.

Submissions from Knee ride:

Spinning armbar
Baseball bat choke

Transitional positions:

Mount (#2) or cross side (#4)

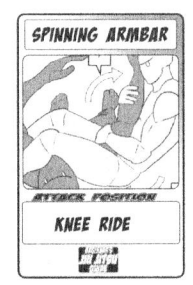

Pg 48   Pg 50

#4 Cross side top: Your opponent has very limited strikes or submissions from this position. It is difficult to strike your opponent in this position but it is a great position to control your opponent and look for submissions.

Submissions from Cross side top:

Kimura
Americana
Spinning armbar

Transitional positions:

Knee ride (#3) or mount (#2): Knee ride is easier to transition to but harder to maintain than mount. North south (#5) is a great escape position if your opponent starts setting up guard recovery.

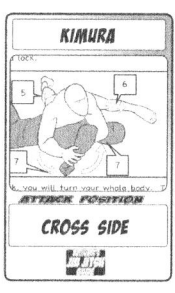 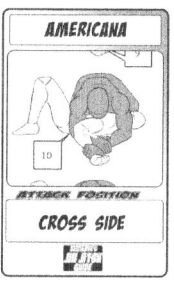 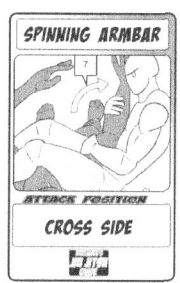

Pg 52   Pg 54   Pg 56

#5 North south: In a no rules fight, you can throw devastating knees to your opponents head from this position. If you can't mount offense from north south, you can easily transition to cross side.

Submissions to attempt from northsouth:

-Armbar
-Paper cutter choke

Transitional positions:

Cross side (#4) is a great place to go if you can't find submissions in north south.

 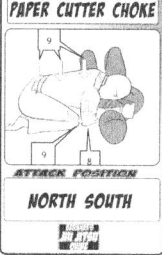

Pg 58   Pg 61

#6 Turtle top: Turtle top is a position that can be difficult to control but if you can, it can be a very strong striking position. Turtle top is the strongest transitional position to back mount.

Transitional positions:

-Back mount (#1) or bulldoze them over to cross side (#4)

Pg 63

#7 Half guard top: In sports Jiu Jitsu, half guard is often a transitional position on your way to pass the guard. In a fight, this could be a fight ending position where you can rain down strikes or finish your opponent with a submission.

Transitional positions:

Cross side (#4)

#8 Guard Top: This is a position where you can throw effective strikes to end the fight or use strikes to set up your guard pass. Leg locks are available if the guard is open, but there is a risk of your opponent getting top position if the leg lock attempt fails.

Submissions to from guard top:

Ankle lock, once the guard is open

Transitional positions:

Cross side (#4) once guard is open

Pg 64

#9 Guard bottom: Although Guard bottom is placed at #9, many Jiu Jitsu fighters thrive in this position. A great guard player can nullify the attackers strikes and set up submissions and sweeps.

Submissions from guard bottom:

Armbar
Kimura
Cross choke

  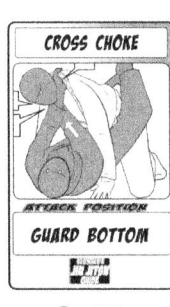

Pg 67   Pg 69   Pg 71

Transitional positions:

Sweep to cross side (#4), mount (#2), knee ride (#3), half guard top (#7) or transition to the #1 position, back mount

#10 Half guard bottom:

When strikes are involved, half guard has to be played very carefully. Even a great half guard player could be in serious trouble if one heavy strike lands. This is not a position that you can slowly set up your offense. You must act immediately and be decisive.

POSITIONS

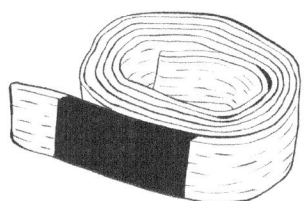

In this chapter, you will see instructions for positions where the characters are described doing movements on just one side. The positions can be done on either side but has been illustrated on just one side for simplicity.

BACK MOUNT

1. Harness: Right arm over your opponent's trapezius, Left arm under your opponent's armpit. Right arm is your attacking arm to attempt chokes with. Your opponent's will grab your right hand to defend the choke. Grab your right hand with your left hand, taking away your opponent's basic defense.

2. Hook both of your legs around your opponents hip line.

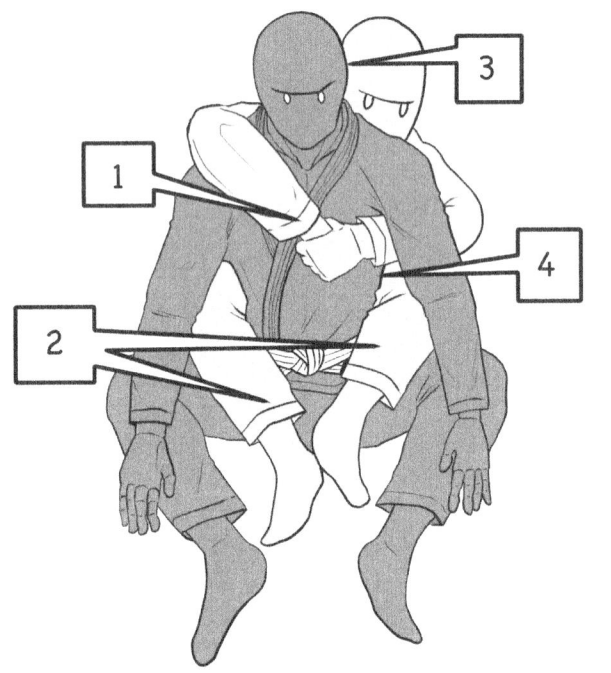

3. Lock the right side of your head with the left back side of your opponent's head. This will help control your opponent's ability to move and it will help avoid accidental head collision.

4. Attach your chest to your opponent's back. Any space here will allow your opponent to turn and escape this position.

5. Here you will be doing 4 things at once to stretch out your opponent. Do this slowly as your opponent may need to tap to the pressure and to make sure you don't harm your training partner with sudden unexpected movement.

A. Drive your arms up to the point where your opponent feels a choke coming on by your right forearm.

B. Drive your legs down.

C. Pull your shoulders back.

D. Arch your back.

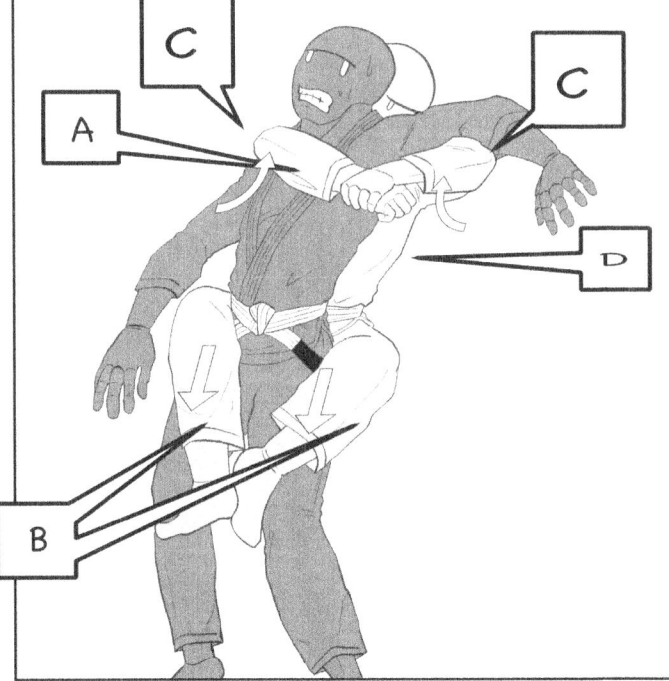

LOW MOUNT

1. Lock your ankles and lift your feet up. Your opponent will most likely step on your feet to unlock them so hide them by lifting them up.

2. Lower your torso down on your opponent with your back straight. If you curve your back, you will take weight and pressure off of your opponent. Bend at your hips and keep your back completely straight.

A. Chest resting on your opponents body.

B. knees should be the only thing touching the ground.

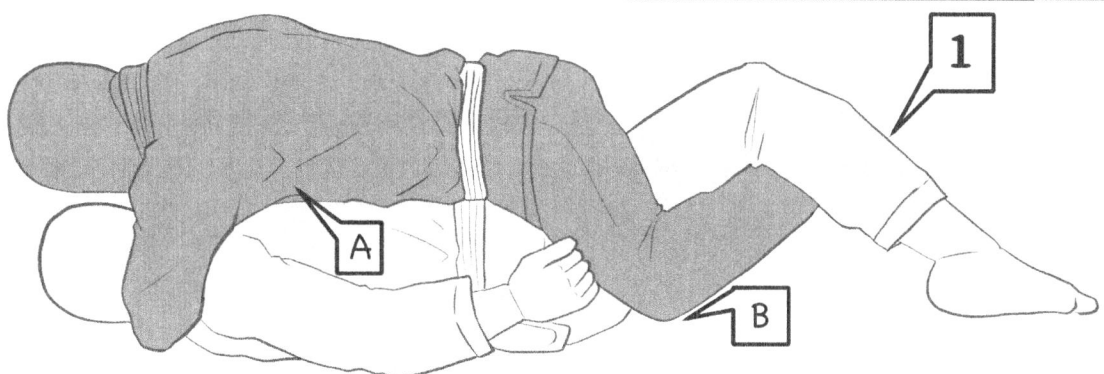

3. Wrap your left arm around your opponent's head. Use your Left shoulder to turn your opponent's face to the right. Left hand gripping your opponent's gi fabric to lock in your cross face. This should make it very difficult for your opponent to bridge you over to your left.

4. Shift your torso to your right to add extra pressure to the cross face.

3. Cross face

5. Post your right hand far to the right. This post will keep you from getting bridged to your right side.

Post far away so it is difficult for your opponent to grab your arm.

KNEE RIDE

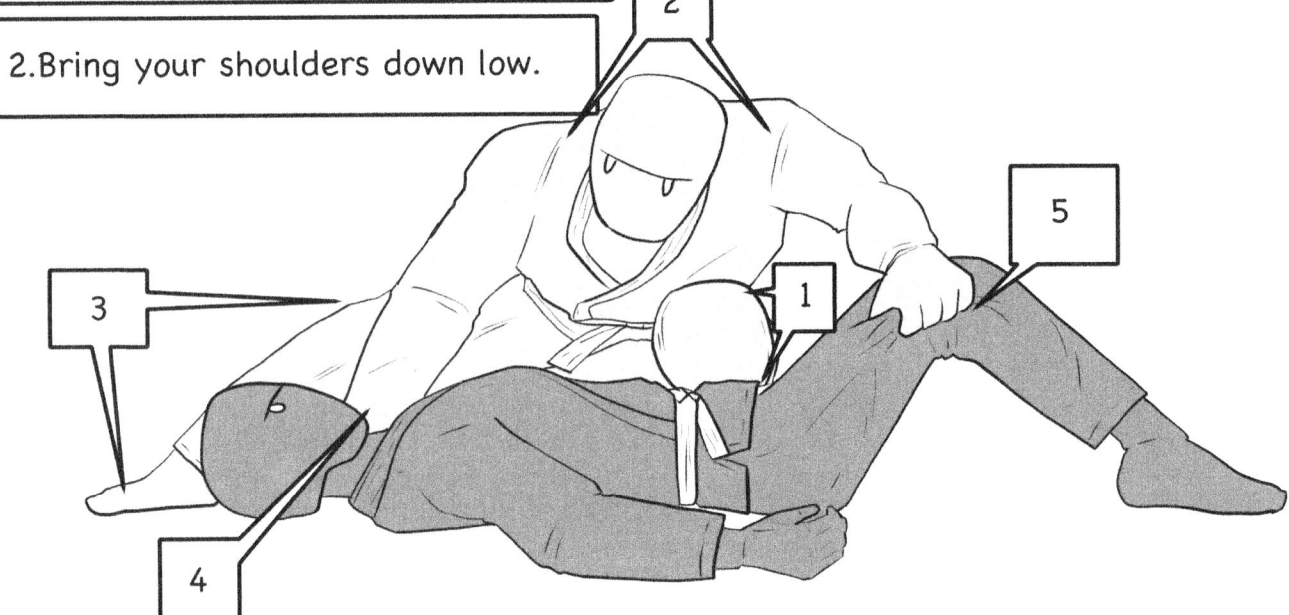

1. Place your left shin all the way across your opponent's stomach. Hook your left foot on your opponent's hip and bring your hips all the way down till your left heel touches your butt.

2. Bring your shoulders down low.

3. Right foot kicks out, near your opponent's head. Knee is pointed up, slightly bent.

4. Grab the near side collar with your right hand. You will use this grip to push your opponent's face away if they attempt to turn towards you. To do this, keep your grip and turn your elbow towards your opponent's face.

5. Grip your opponent's gi pants on the far side leg. If they try to turn away from you, pull the leg to bring them back.

In the beginning, knee ride is a difficult position to control. Knee ride will become much more effective if you learn the transition from knee ride to mount, cross side and north south.

CROSS SIDE

1. Underhook with your right arm. Put your right elbow on the ground for balance. Left arm wraps your opponent's head with shoulder turning your opponent's face away from you. This cross face will keep your opponent from turning into you.

2. Place your left knee by your opponent's head. This will bring your torso over your opponent's shoulder line, ensuring that you are blocking your opponent's shoulder line, trapping 3 points, both shoulders and head.

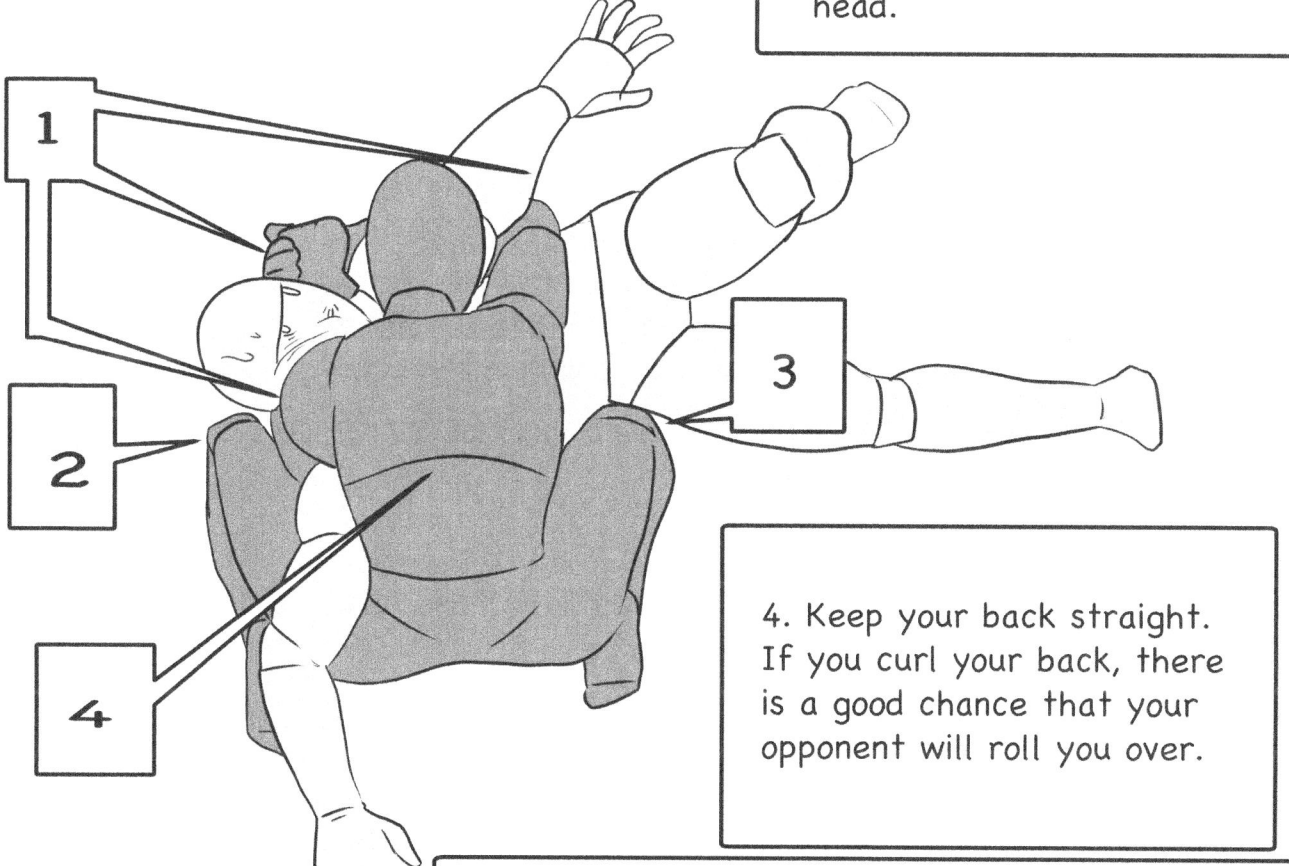

3. Right knee by your opponent's hip. This will assist your cross face in keeping your opponent's from turning into you.

4. Keep your back straight. If you curl your back, there is a good chance that your opponent will roll you over.

Don't think of this position as a place where you use your body weight to hold your opponent down. Think of it as a position where you block and lock your opponent down. With proper structure, Your opponent will feel like they are trapped in a box. A very small box.

NORTH SOUTH

1. Shift left side of your body to the side of your opponent's face, turning their face away from you. Move your body weight off center to the right. This will make it difficult for your opponent to roll you over.

2. Lower your head and body as much as possible. Contour your body to your opponent's body. If your head or body comes up, your opponent will most likely push you off. Stay low.

3. Overhook your opponent's arm with your left arm. Bring your forearm as deep into the armpit as you can. Left hand is placed on opponent's body, palm down.

4. Spread your legs wide to make it difficult for your opponent to roll you over. It maybe tempting to come off your knees to pressure your opponent. Keep your knees as low as possible.

TURTLE TOP

1. Attach the right side of your body to your opponent's side. This will look very much like the knee ride position we covered earlier.

2. Your right knee will be driving into your opponent slightly.

3. Bring your Hips down low. Lean on your opponent but don't place your weight on top of your opponent as they will be able to roll you with ease.

4. Seatbelt. Right Hand will reach to the far side to grab belt or Gi fabric.

5. Left hand will grab the back of the collar.

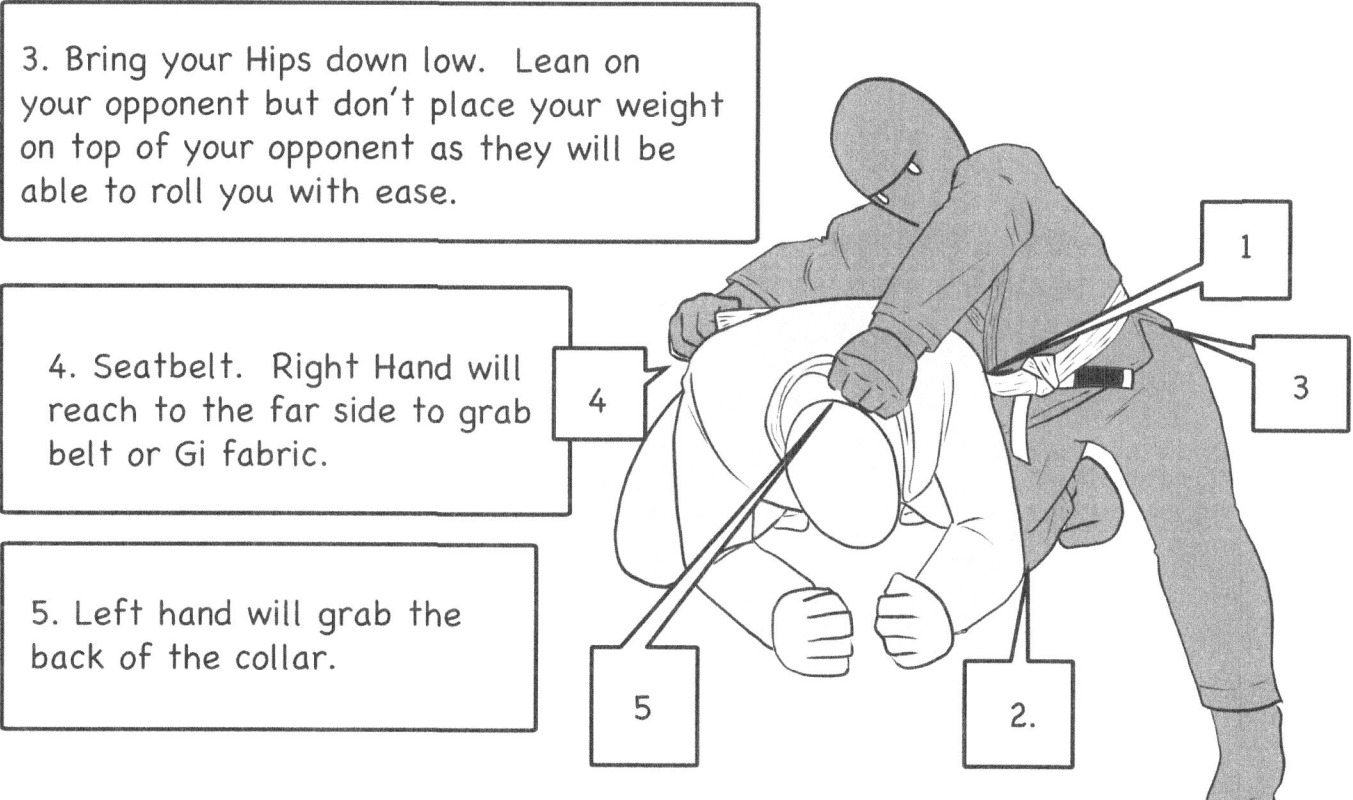

HALF GUARD TOP

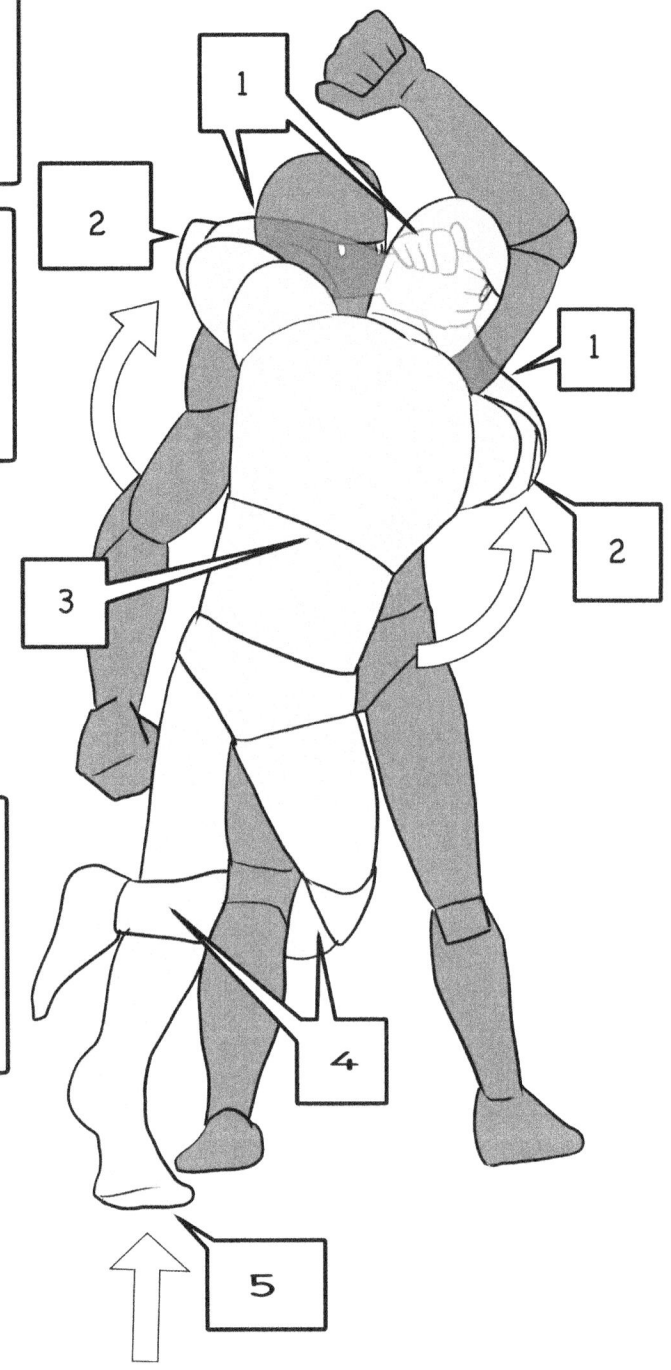

1. With your right arm, underhook your opponent's far arm. Your left arm will wrap around your opponent's head and cross face with your left shoulder. Lock your hands together.

2. Open up your elbows so it will keep you balanced. If your opponent moves side to side, plant on whichever elbow they are turning towards.

3. Keep your back straight. If you curve you back, your opponent will be able to turn and escape much easier.

4. Triangle: Your right leg will go under your opponent's leg and the end of your shin will lock on behind your left knee to make a triangle.

5. Drive your left toes into the mat. This is the only driving force that can propel you forward to add pressure to your head and arm control.

GUARD TOP

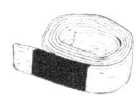 

1. There are many grip options. The safest one to start with is the double lapel grip. Left hand grips the left lapel, right hand grips the right lapel. Grip as far as you can while your elbows stay under your shoulders. This simple rule of keeping your elbows under your shoulders will keep you from getting into lots of trouble. It is very difficult for your opponent to catch submissions or off balance you for sweeps if they can not get you to extend your arm or open your elbows.

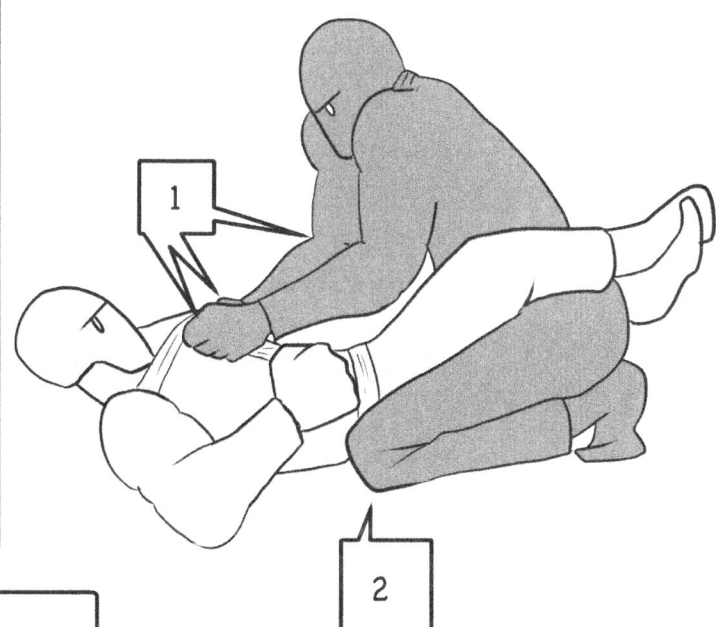

2. Place your knees on the outside of your opponent's hips. This will keep you in tune with your opponent's hip movements and will make it difficult for your opponent to move their hips.

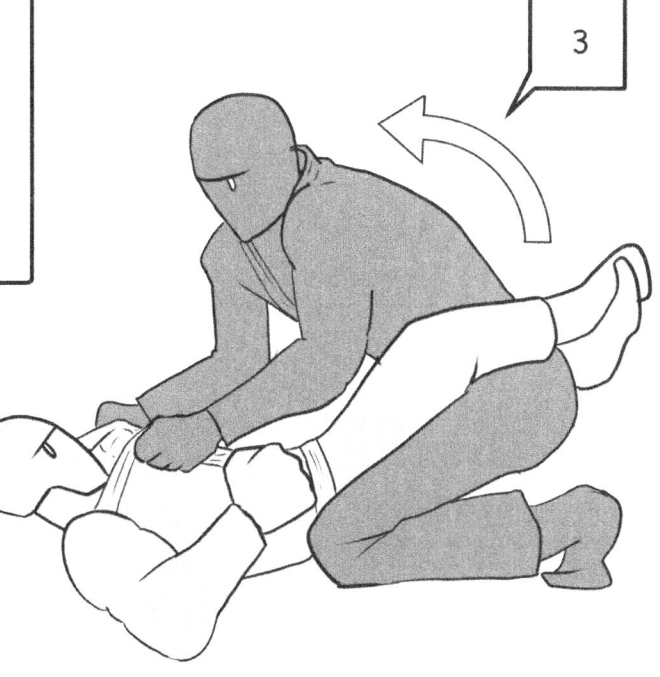

3. If you need to reach further, try shifting your whole body forward instead of reaching with just your arms.

GUARD BOTTOM

1. Bring hips close into your opponent.

2. Intertwine your ankles tight.

3. With your left hand, grip your opponent's collar on your right side (Cross collar grip).

4. With your right hand, grip the outside of your opponent's sleeve.

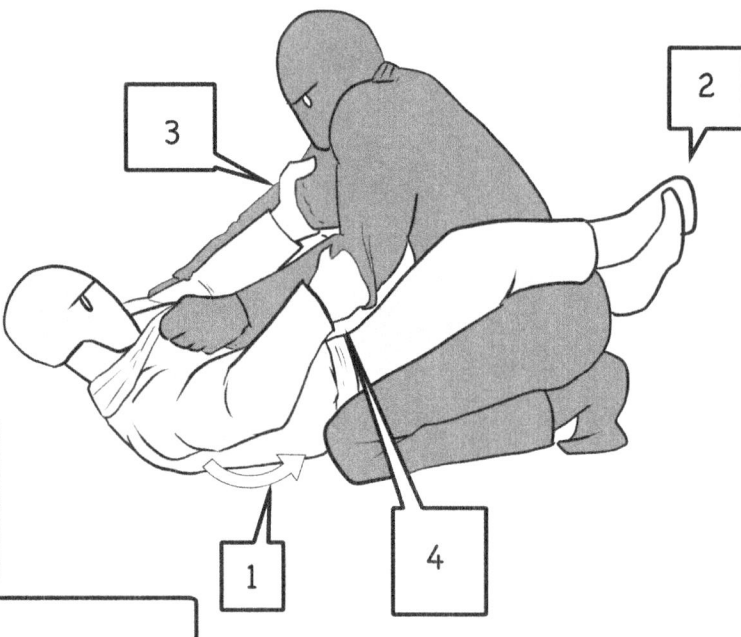

When your opponent is in your closed guard, they have to open your guard before they can mount much offense. Your goal here is to get the best grips you can while your opponent is trapped in your closed guard. Break your opponent's posture by pulling them forward using your grips and legs. Get in the habit of breaking down your opponent's posture before attacking.

5. Once you have maintained closed guard for a period of time, you can play with open guard. Keep the same grips but transition your feet on your opponent's hips. Apply push pull tension to break your opponent's posture.

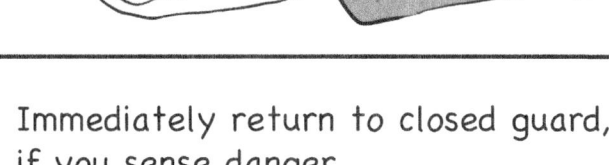

Immediately return to closed guard, if you sense danger.

HALF GUARD BOTTOM

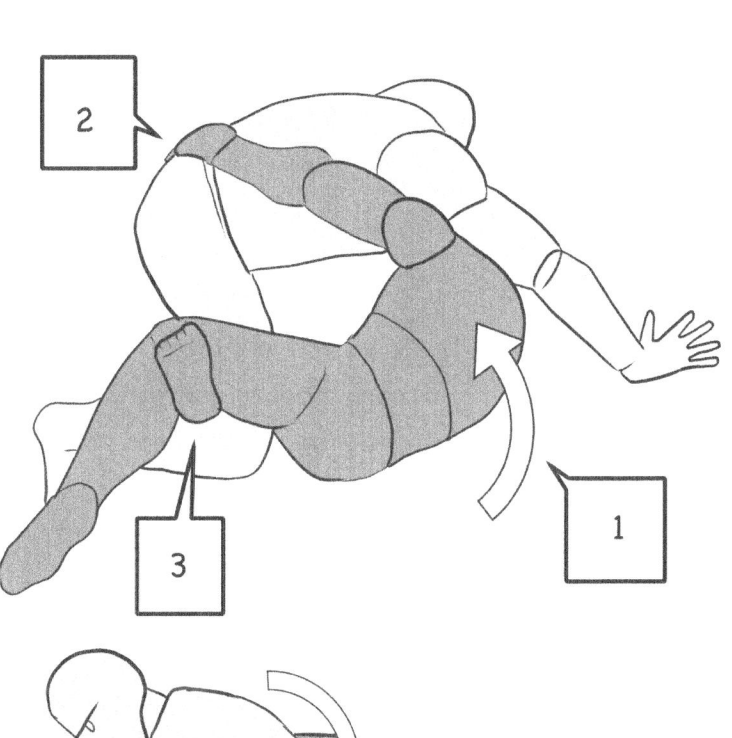

1. Turn sideways facing your opponent.

2. Seatbelt: Underhook with left arm. Left hand grabbing the far hip of your opponent.

3. Triangle: Right foot hooks behind your left knee. Turn your left knee in to lock your leg position. This will make it difficult for your opponent to pull their leg out.

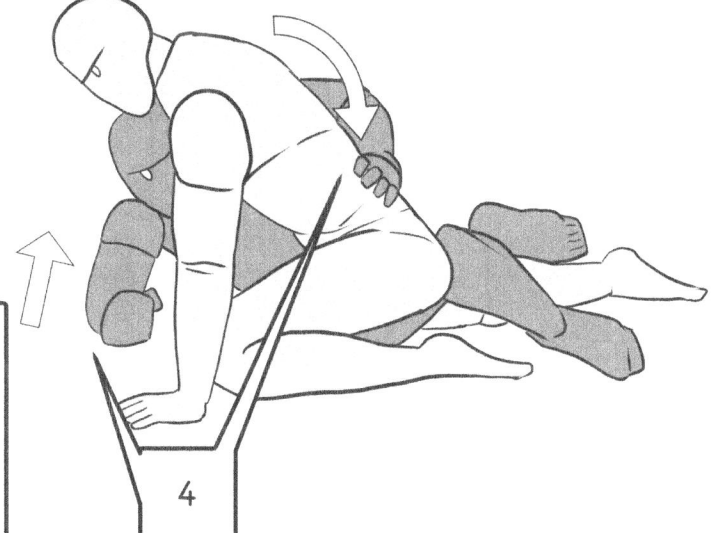

4. Come up to you right elbow, scooting your way around to your opponent's back.

SUBMISSIONS

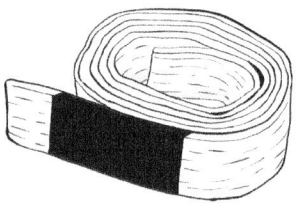

In this chapter, you will see instructions for positions where the characters are described doing movements on just one side. The positions can be done on either side but has been illustrated on just one side for simplicity.

REAR NAKED CHOKE

1. Tighten your harness (arm positions).

2. Tighten your hooks (Leg positions).

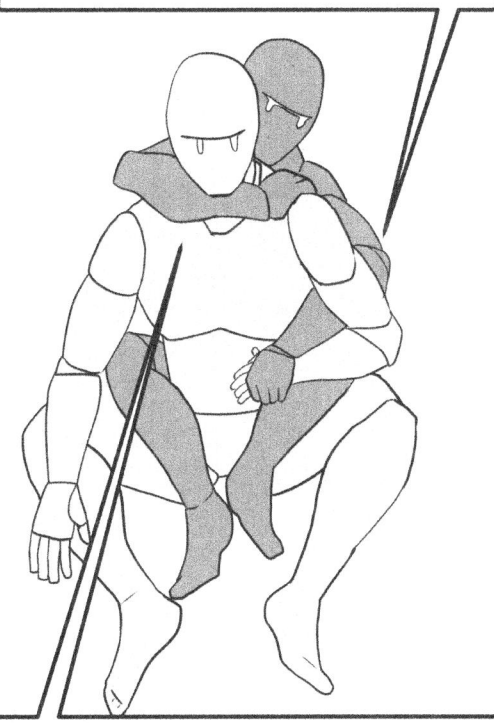

3. Left hand grabs your opponent's left hand to take away their defense.

4. Right forearm goes under your opponent's neck and right hand grabs your opponent's trapezius.

REAR NAKED CHOKE

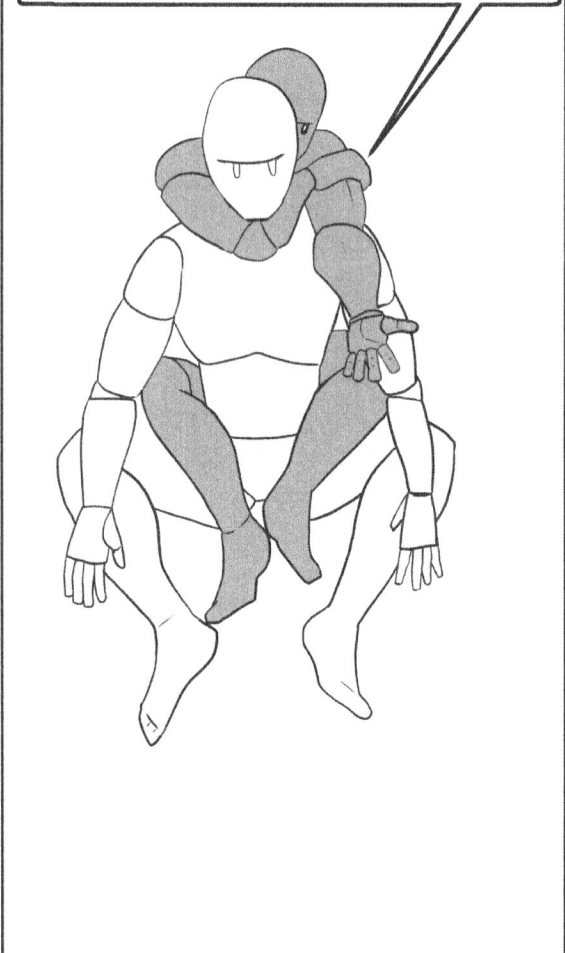

5. Right hand grabs your left bicep as deep as possible. Right elbow should be aligned with your opponent's chin

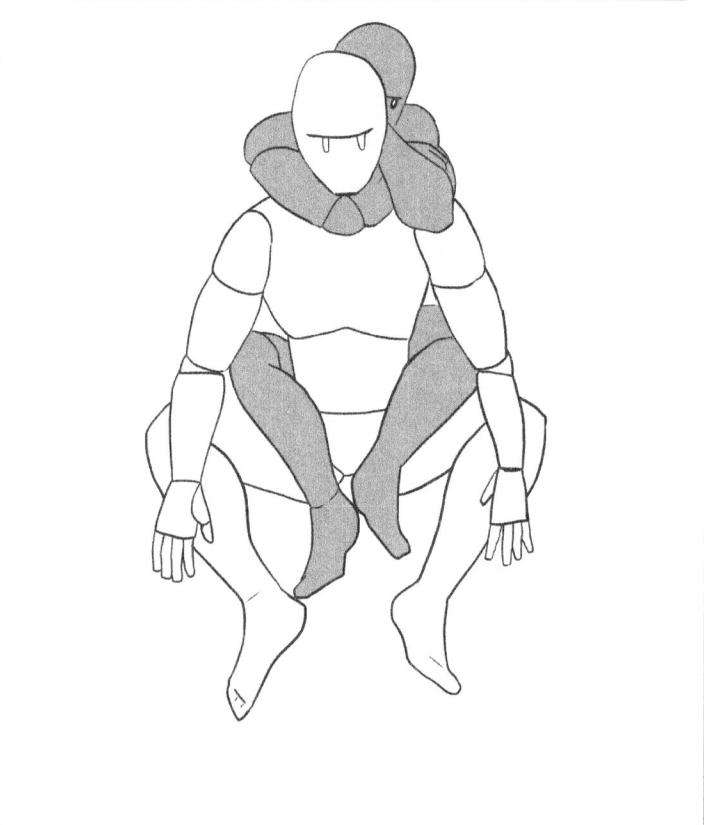

6. Left hand comes behind your opponent's head, palm down, reaching towards your right shoulder. Squeeze slowly with your arms. With your left arm, push your opponent's head towards your right elbow to complete the choke.

ARMBAR

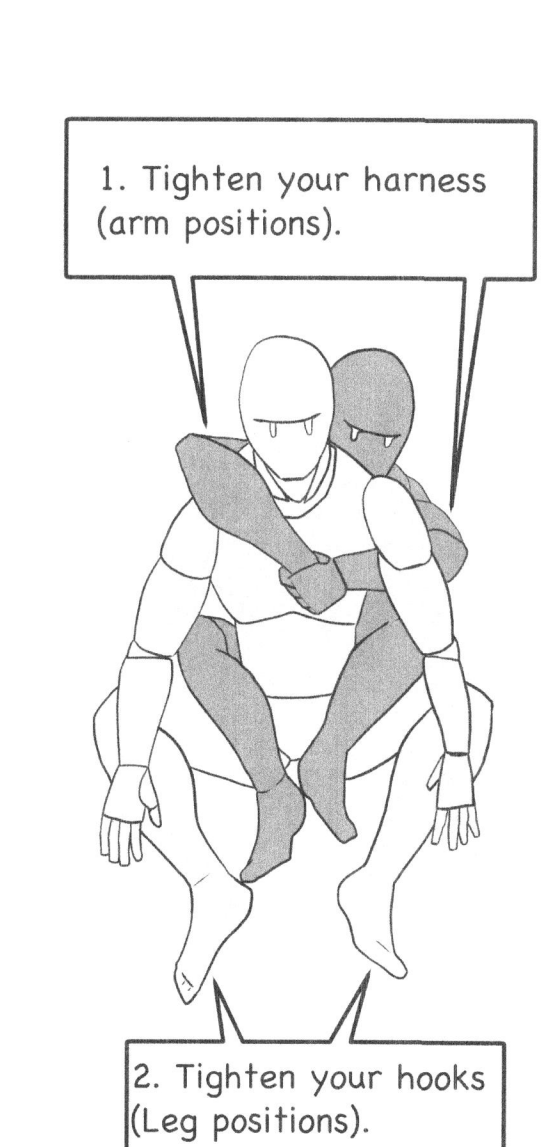

1. Tighten your harness (arm positions).

2. Tighten your hooks (Leg positions).

3. Right forearm drives into the left side of your opponent's neck. Right hand grabs your left wrist.

ARMBAR

4. Right foot goes to your opponent's right hip. Left leg goes across your opponent's stomach.

5. Fall to your left side. As you are falling, create tension by pushing your opponents neck with your right arm and pulling on your opponent's left arm. As you are falling, bring your right leg over your opponent's head.

ARMBAR

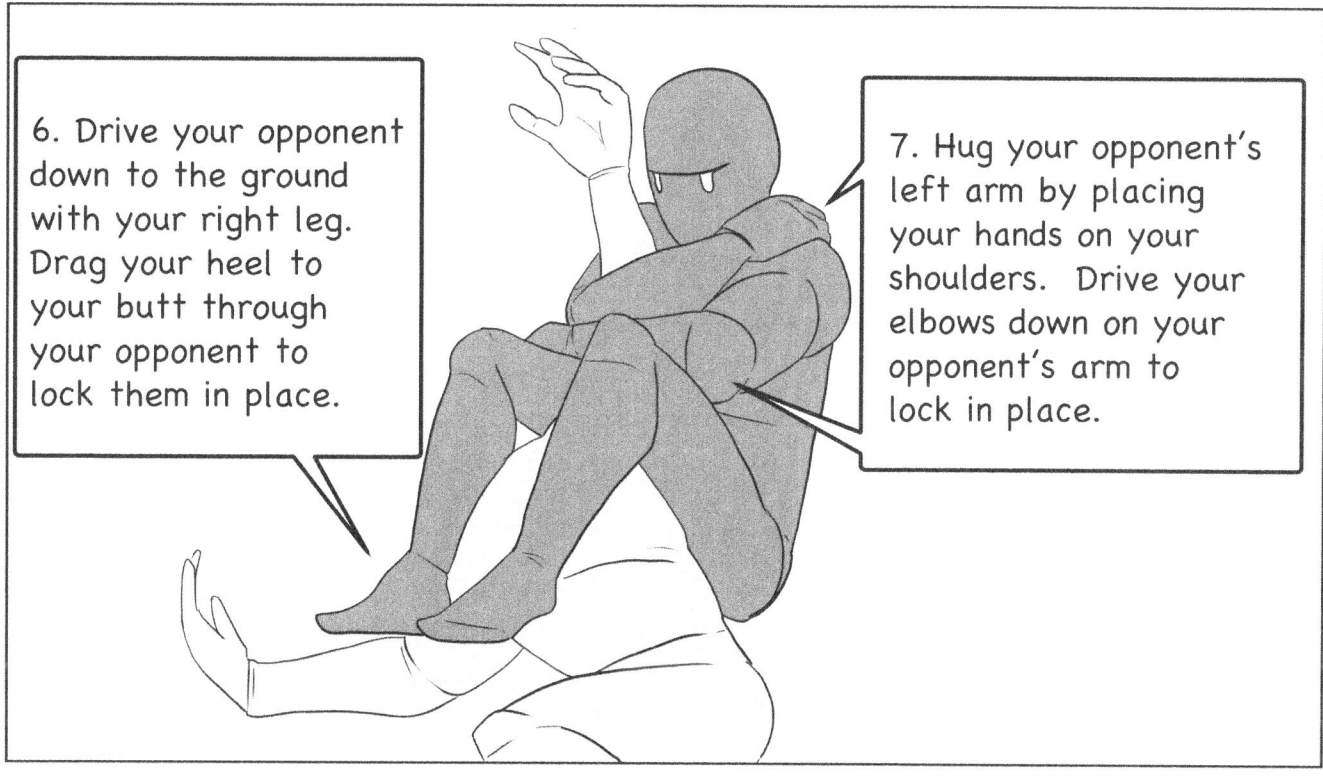

6. Drive your opponent down to the ground with your right leg. Drag your heel to your butt through your opponent to lock them in place.

7. Hug your opponent's left arm by placing your hands on your shoulders. Drive your elbows down on your opponent's arm to lock in place.

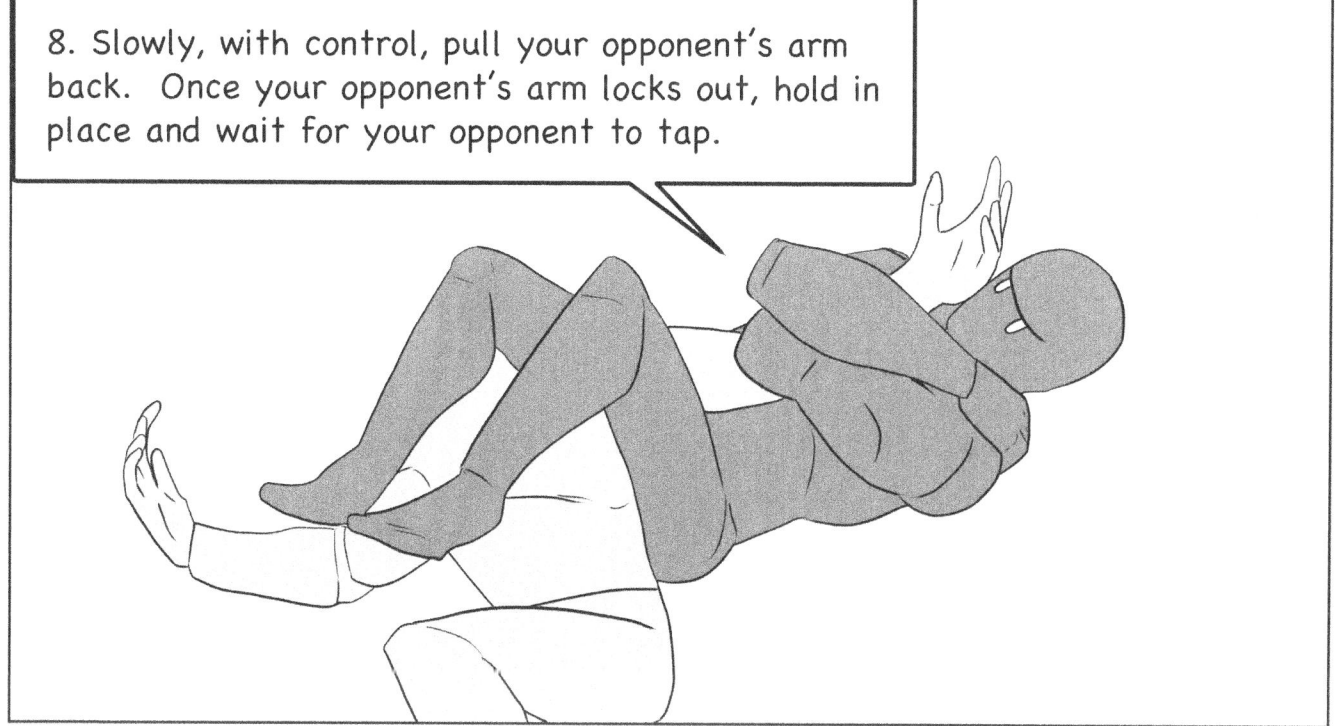

8. Slowly, with control, pull your opponent's arm back. Once your opponent's arm locks out, hold in place and wait for your opponent to tap.

SLIDING LAPEL CHOKE

1. Tighten your harness (arm positions).

2. Tighten your hooks (Leg positions).

3. Right hand grips into your opponent's left side collar, thumb in, as deep as possible. This grip should be so deep that if you were to pull, you can choke your opponent with just your right hand.

4. Left hand grabs your opponent's left hand to take away his defense.

SLIDING LAPEL CHOKE

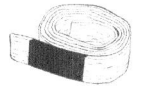 

5. Left hand switches to your opponent's left side lapel in the middle. Pull the lapel down with left hand while right hand choke grip readjusts further up.

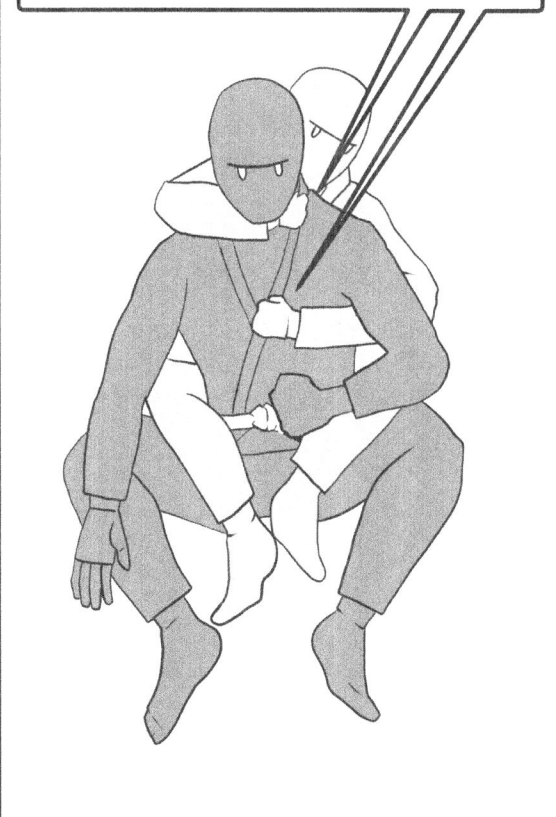

6. Left hand switches to the right side lapel in the center of lapel. Pull the right side lapel to get the slack out of the lapel. Continue pulling with the left hand as you add pulling motion with your right hand to complete the choke.

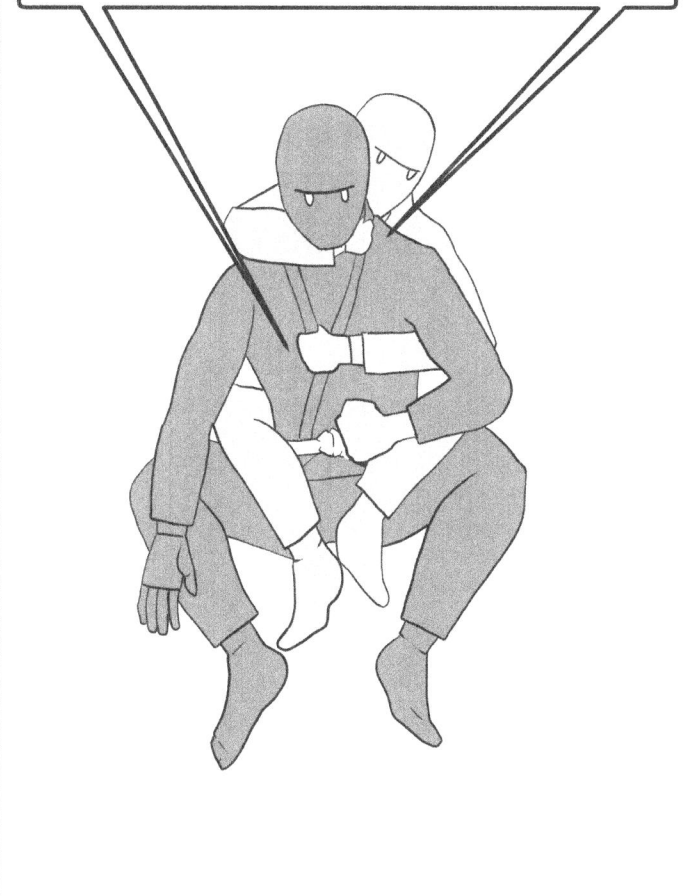

MOUNT CROSS CHOKE

1. Left hand opens opponent's same side lapel.

2. Slide right hand into lapel by the neck, as deep as possible. Pull with your left hand as you slide your right hand in to get rid of slack.

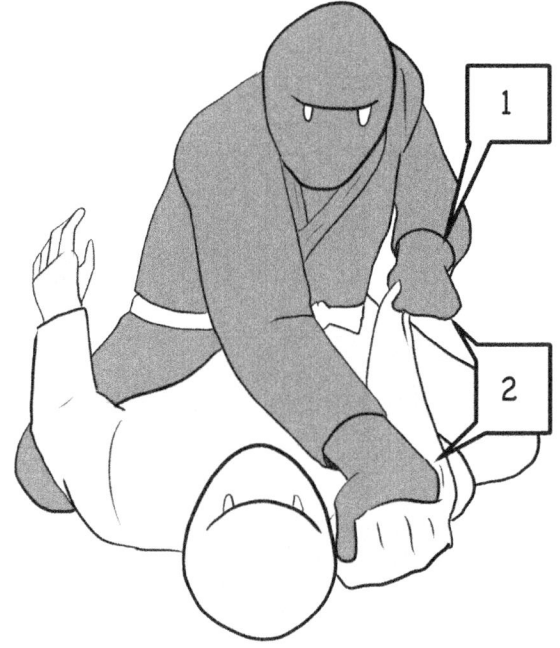

3. Fold your body down with back straight. Place left elbow by opponent's head on the right side.

4. Push opponent's head to the left with your elbow.

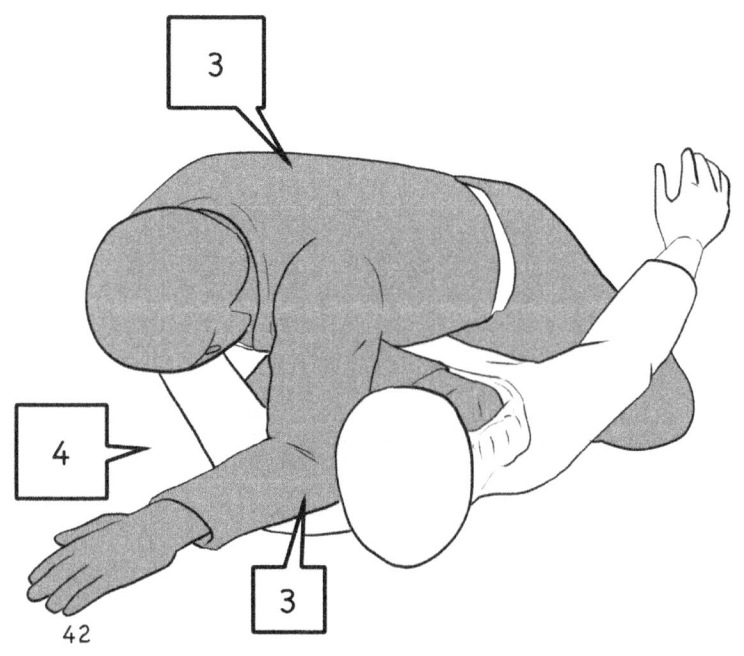

MOUNT CROSS CHOKE

5. Drag your left elbow up, turning your opponent's face to their right.

6. with your left hand, grab the Gi fabric as close to your opponent's neck as possible.

7. Attach your elbows to your ribs. Tighten your grips.

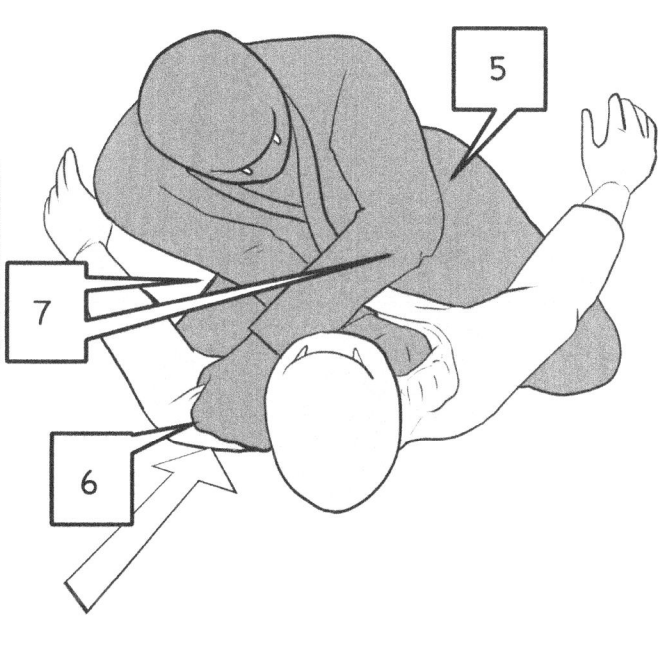

8. Turn your wrist towards your opponent's neck, put your head to the left of your opponent's head. Pull with both hands to finish the choke.

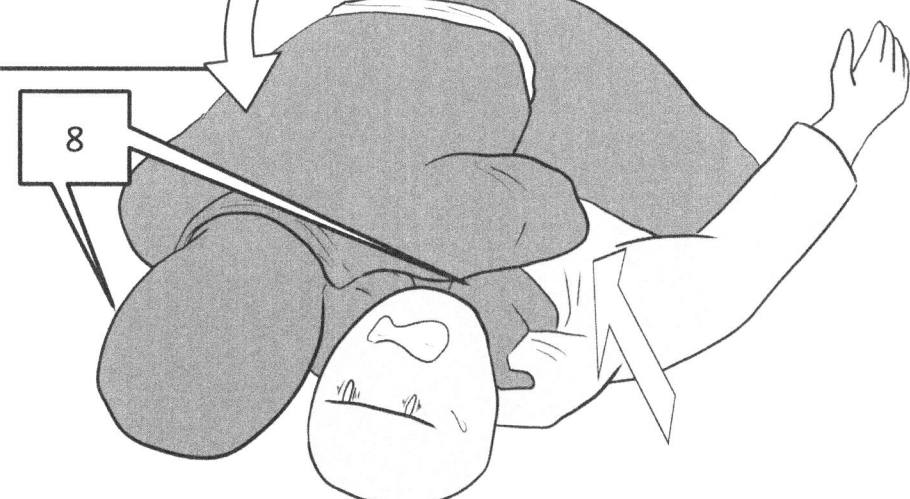

MOUNT ARMBAR

1. Since catching armbar from mount is very difficult, we will start with the scenario that we are holding mount the way it was shown in page 25. From there, if your opponent commits to pushing you off like the way it is illustrated, it is your cue to go for the armbar.

2. When your opponent pushes, left hand comes around your opponent's right arm. Your right hand comes between your opponent's arms towards the center of the chest.

3. Put your hands together and shift your weight into your hands. As the weight shifts from your legs and hips into your hands, your hips and legs should move freely. Spin to the left.

4. Your left knee will be right by your opponent's head. Your right leg will be staying behind by your opponent's left hip.

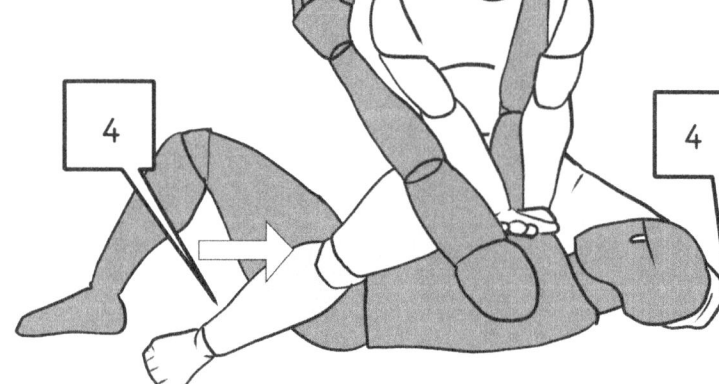

MOUNT ARMBAR

5. Keep pressing your weight into your hands. Move your right leg into the armpit of your opponent.

6. Transfer your weight from your hands to your right thigh by shifting your right shoulder towards your opponent's left hip. This should lighten up the weight of your left leg. Move your left leg over your opponent's head.

7. Hug your opponent's arm near you, sit on the ground slowly with control. Pinch your knees tight together to lock up your opponent's arm. Bring your heels towards you to lock up your opponent's head and torso. Pull your opponent's arm back slowly till it locks out.

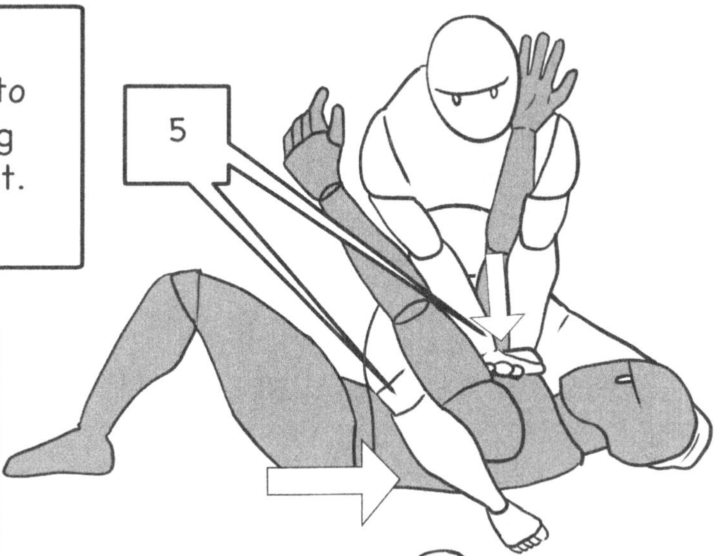

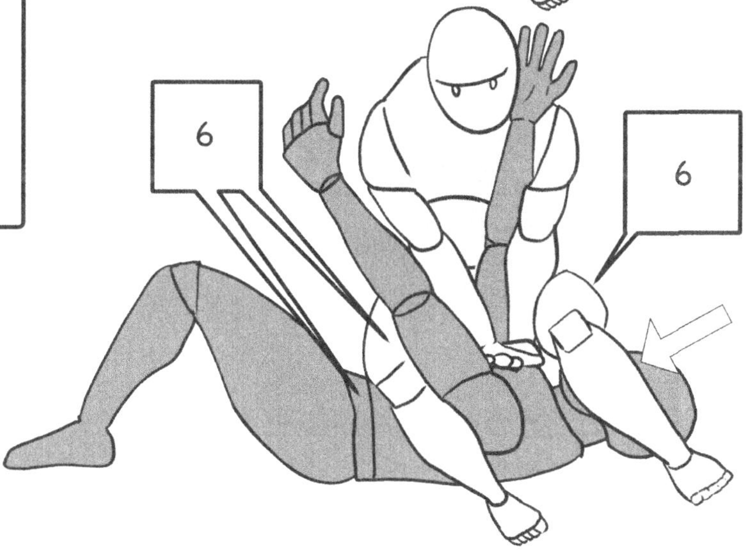

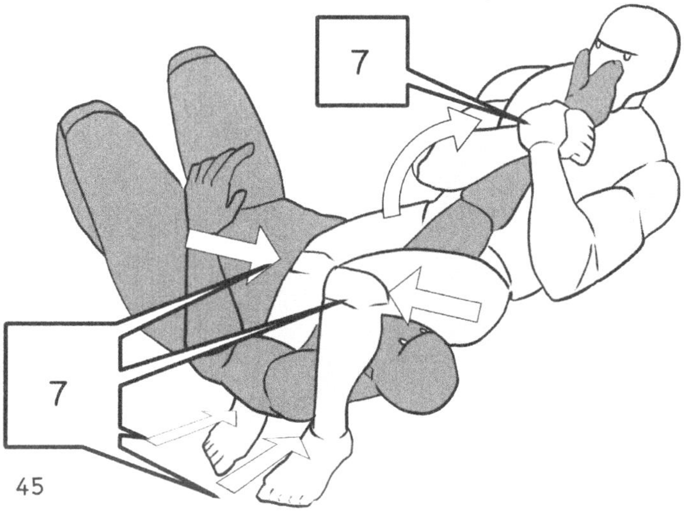

MOUNT AMERICANA

1. Americana is a great way to open up an opponent who has gone into complete defense mode. Grab the hand and elbow of the top arm with both hands. Push the hand down next to their head. Push by transferring your body weight into your hands.

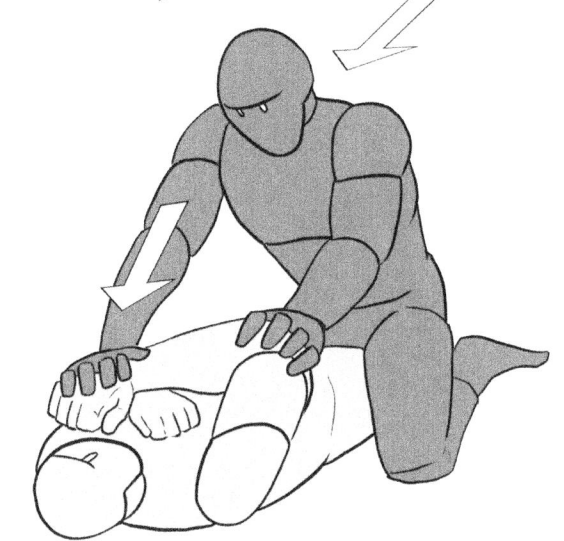

2. Next, push your opponent's elbow to the ground as much as you can.

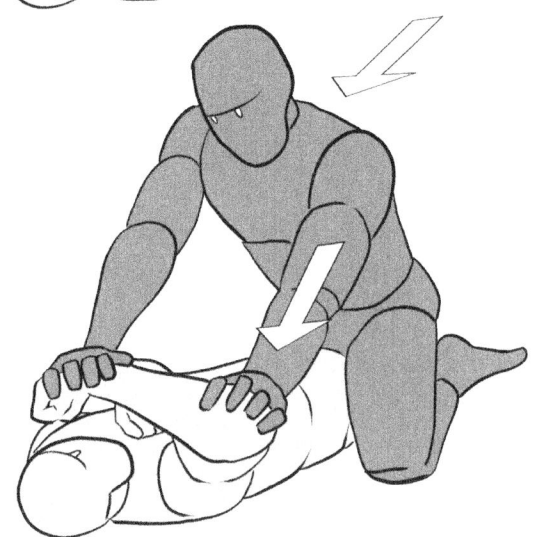

3. Go back to pushing your opponent's hand down. Repeat this process until your opponent's hand and elbow is all the way down to the ground.

MOUNT AMERICANA

4. Place your right elbow next to your opponent's head.

5. Slide your left arm under your opponent's arm, grip your wrist.

6. Pin your opponent's wrist to the ground by driving your hands down. This will tighten the Americana lock.

7. Drag your opponent's elbow down next to their hip.

8. Keep your opponent's wrist pinned to the ground.

9. Slowly lift your opponent's elbow with your left elbow until the elbow locks in place.

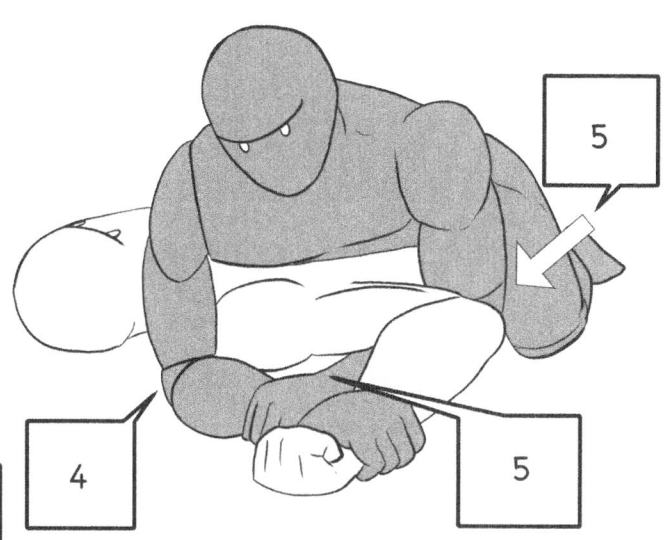

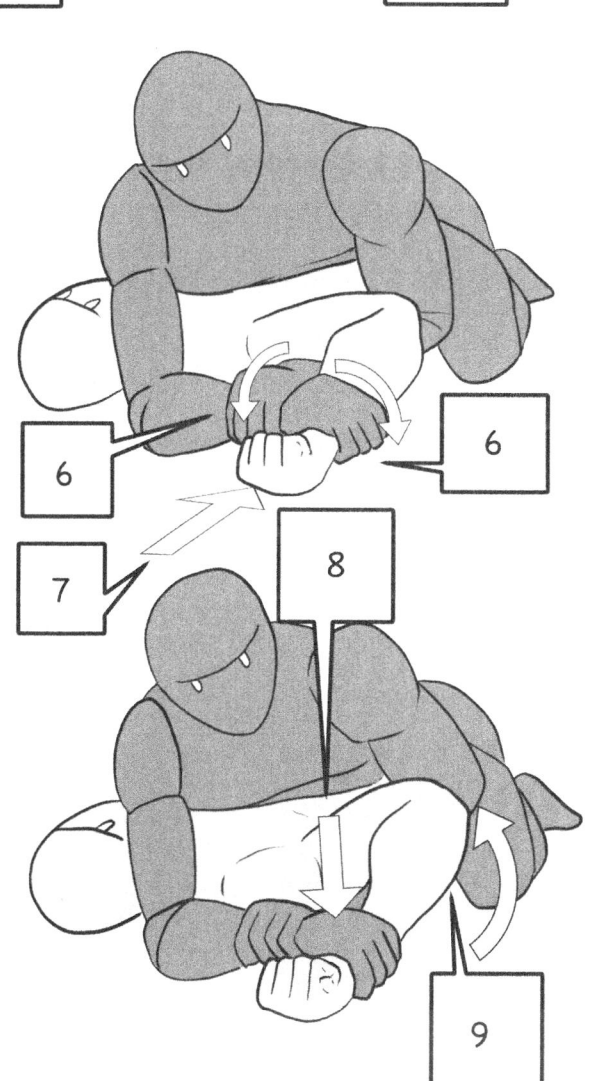

 KNEERIDE SPINNING  ARMBAR

1. From knee ride position, your left hand underhooks your opponent's far side arm.

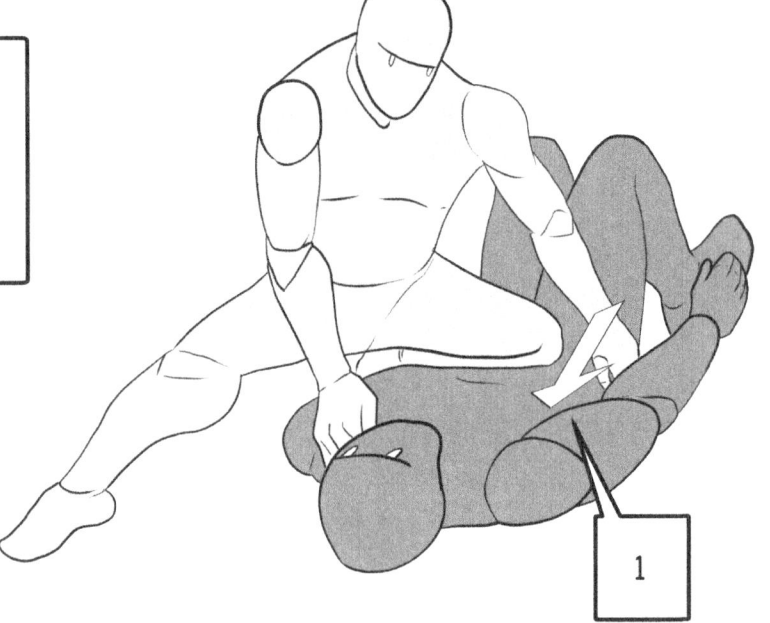

2. Grab the shoulder as deep as possible and pull up. Simultaneously, push your opponent's head down to create tension.

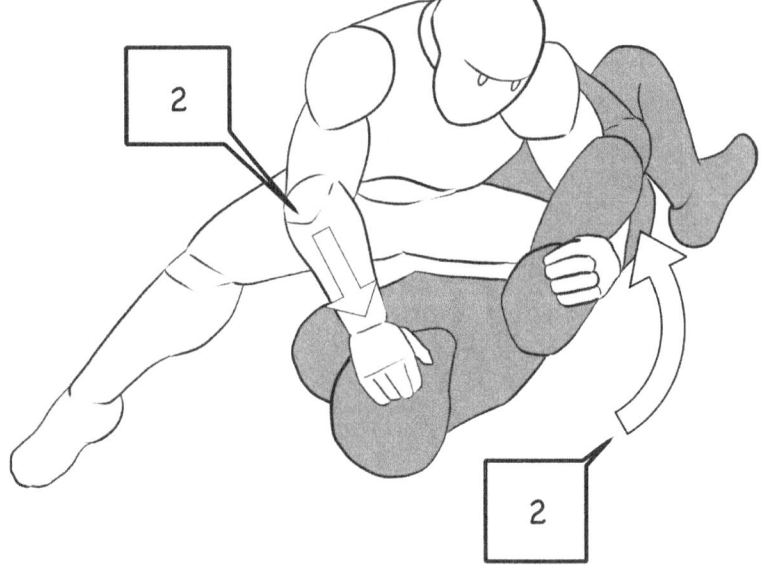

KNEERIDE SPINNING ARMBAR

3. Spin to the other side of your opponent's body. Stay off of your knees.

4. Sit down as you pull your opponent's arm to you.

5. Bring your hips under your opponent as much as possible.

6. Bring your right leg over your opponent's torso. Bring your heels in to pull your opponent into you.

7. Hug your opponent's arm. Slowly pull back till the arm locks out.

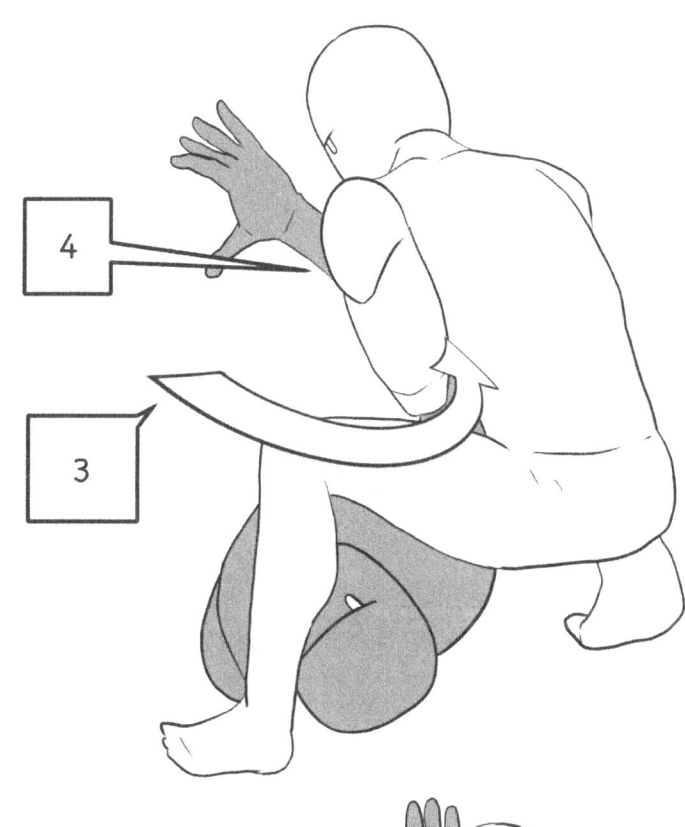

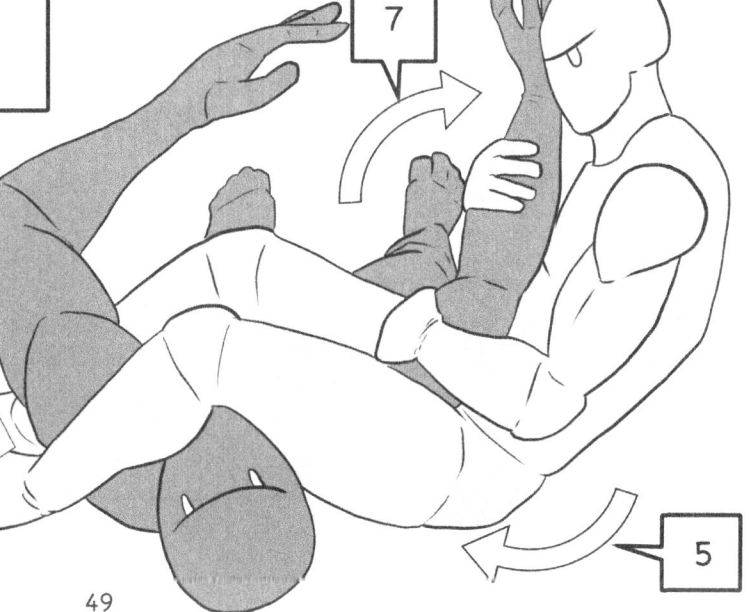

 KNEERIDE BASEBALL  CHOKE

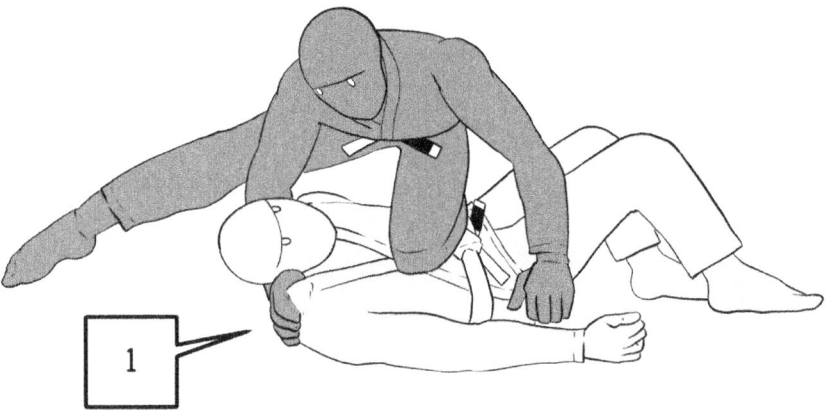

1. Bring your right hand under your opponent's neck. Grip the collar just past the neck with your thumb inside the collar, four fingers out.

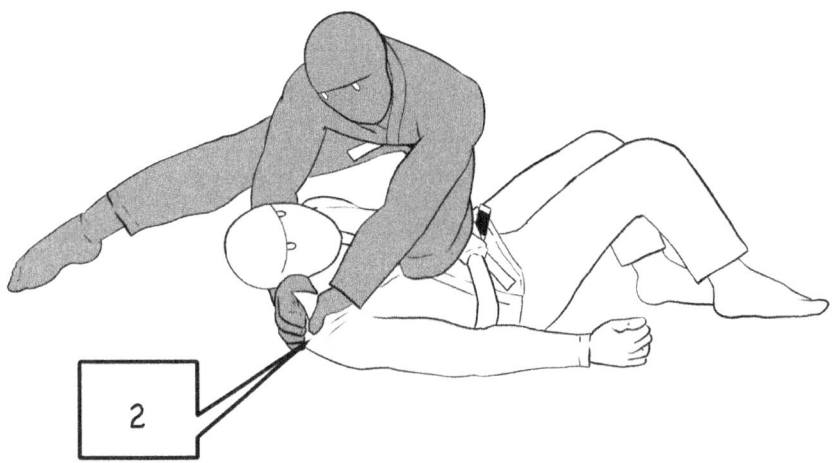

2. Your left hand will go into the collar right next to the right hand, four fingers in, thumb out. Grip tightly.

KNEERIDE BASEBALL CHOKE

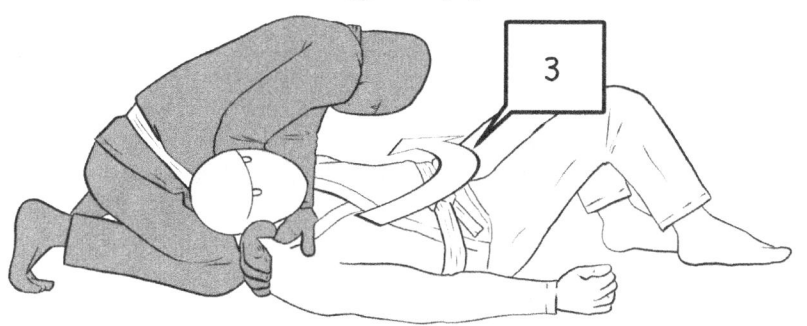

3. Spin to the left into a seated position. As you spin, your left forearm will go into your opponent's throat.

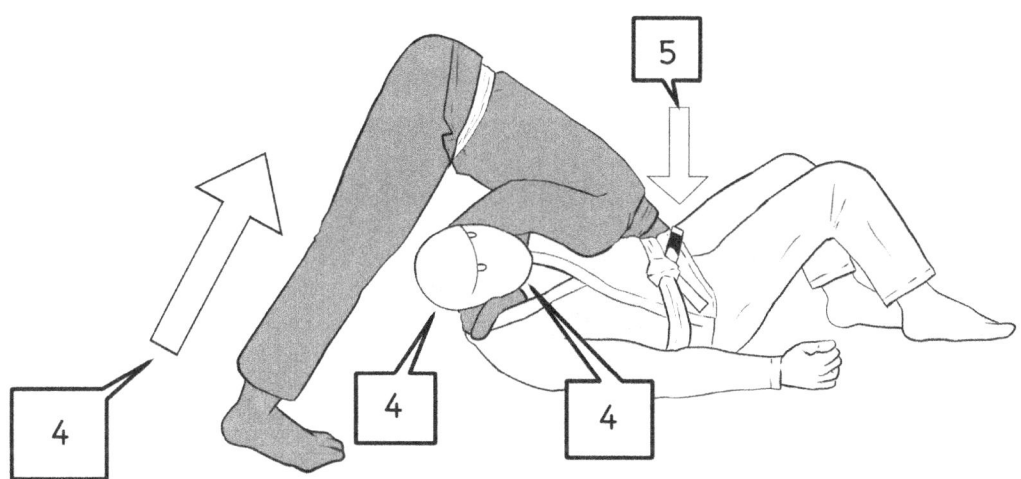

4. Keep driving your forearm into the throat. Drive your hips up and push your right forearm into the back of your opponent's head. This will push your opponent's head into the choke.

5. Put your head by your opponent's hip to prevent them from turning away from the choke.

CROSS SIDE TOP KIMURA

1. You can look for the kimura lock from cross side position anytime your opponent's left hand is past the right side of your head. Before you attack the kimura, Pull your opponent in tight to you, keep your back flat and hips down.

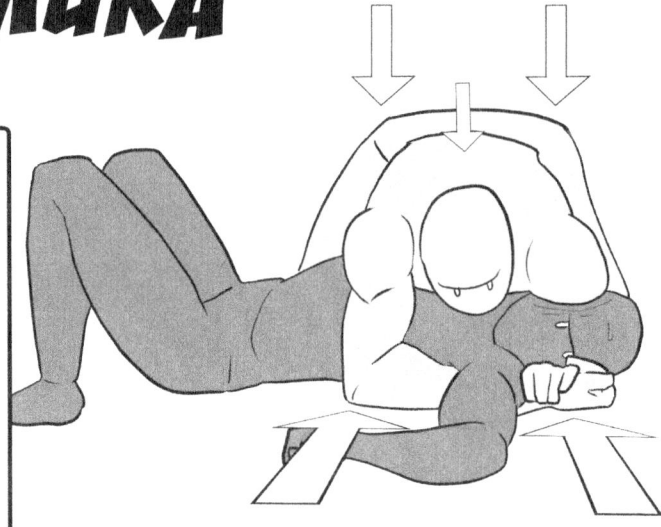

2. Bring your left elbow to the other side of your opponent's head. Lock your hands to your wrists and pull your opponents into you again.

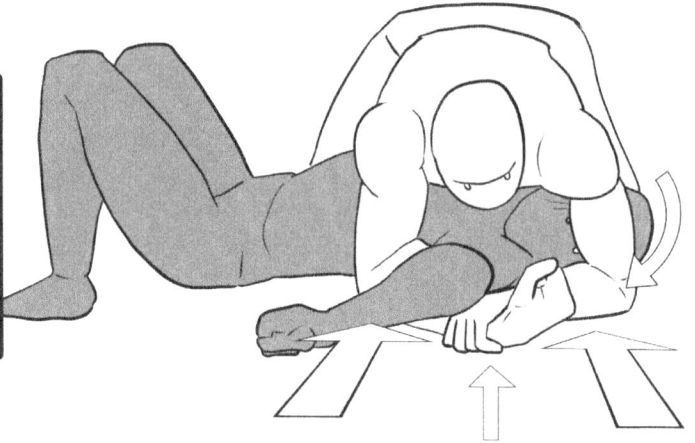

3. Grab your opponent's left hand and wrist with your right hand. Pin it all the way to the ground. Next, put your right elbow down to the ground. This will separate your opponent's arm from their torso, making it harder to defend the kimura lock.

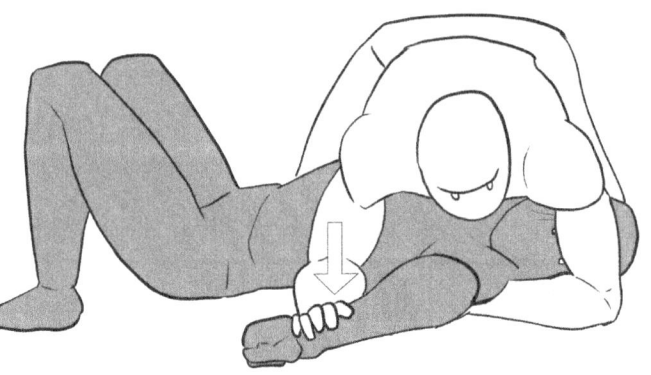

CROSS SIDE TOP KIMURA

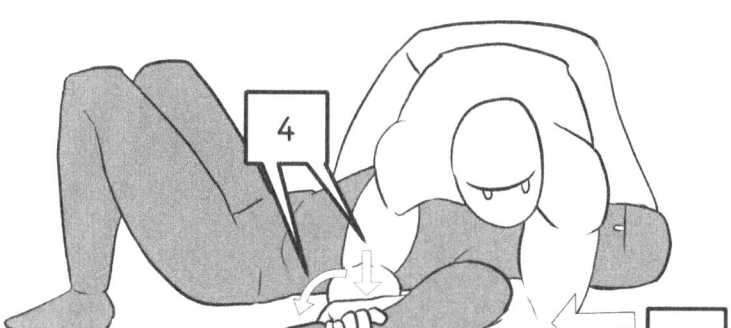

4. Slide your left hand under your opponent's right elbow. Grab your right wrist with your left hand. Roll your hands down to tighten the lock. This should bring your wrists up and your fingers down. If your lock feels barely locked in, shift your torso forward with a flat back to get closer to your kimura lock.

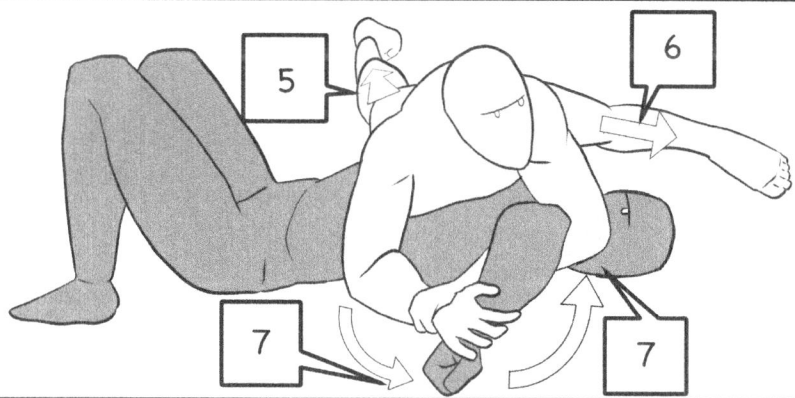

5. To finish the kimura lock, you will turn your whole body. The tighter your hands and body position, the less you will need to move to finish this move. First, kick your right leg behind you, dropping your right hip low to the ground.

6. Kick your left leg to the left side, knee off the ground. Dig your toes into the ground as you will be providing the power to lift your opponents shoulder from your toes.

7. Slowly, lift your left hip up slightly, drag your opponent's elbow up with your left elbow. Smear your opponent's hand under your opponent's elbow with your right hand until the arm locks out.

CROSS SIDE TOP AMERICANA

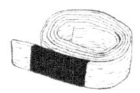

1. When your opponent frames on your throat with their forearm, it is your opportunity to setup your americana.

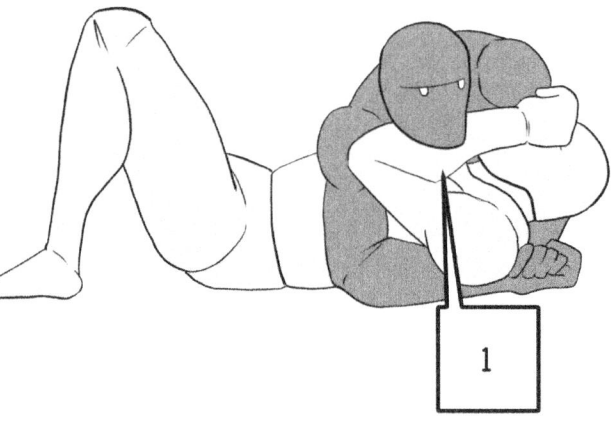

2. Turn your head towards your opponent's head to ease the pressure to your neck from your opponent's forearm.

3. Grab your opponent's shoulder with your right hand.

4. Put your right shoulder in front of your opponent's left arm.

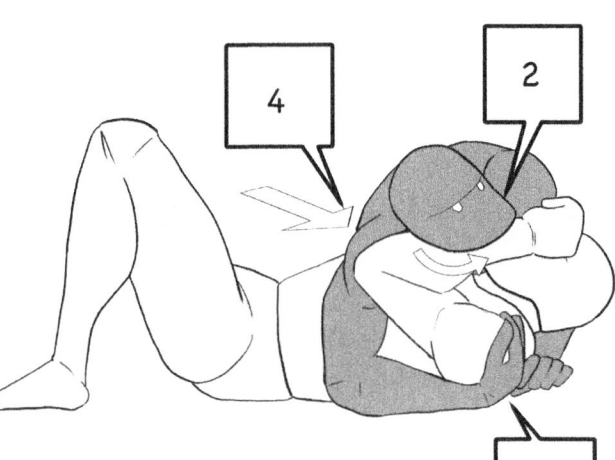

5. Drive your opponent's arm to the ground with your right shoulder. To power your shoulder, drive off of your toes. Keep your legs wide for balance.

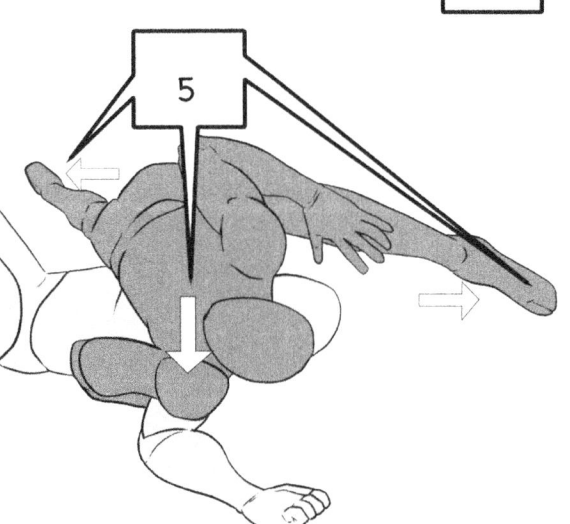

CROSS SIDE TOP AMERICANA

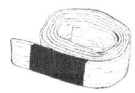 

6. Use your free left hand to pin your opponent's left hand.

7. Bring your knees down. Keep your knees apart, keep your back flat.

8. Thread your right hand under your opponent's arm and grab your left wrist.

9. Tighten your grips by rolling your hands down, wrist up, fingers down.

10. Slowly bring your opponent's left elbow down to their left hip. Be very careful as your opponent may have to tap at this point.

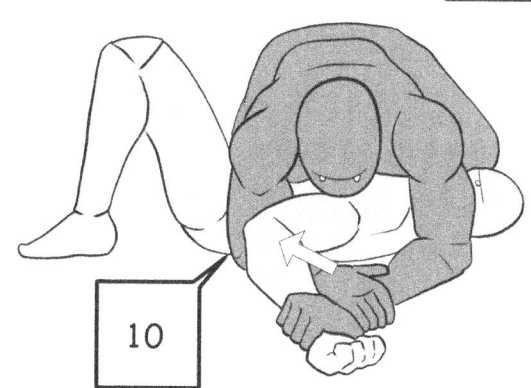

11. Keep your opponent's left hand pinned to the ground. Slowly lift your opponent's left elbow up by lifting your elbow until it locks out.

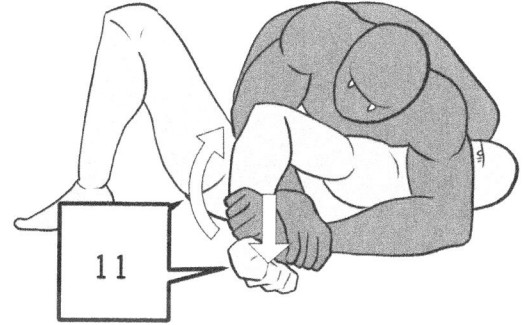

CROSS SIDE SPINNING ARMBAR

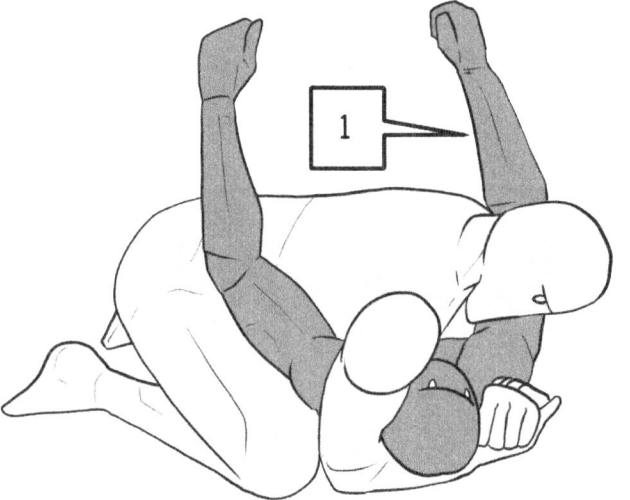

1. Keep track of your opponent's right arm with the left side of your head. If your opponent's arm switches from the left side of your head to the right, your spinning armbar option will be gone.

2. Grab your opponent's right shoulder with your left hand, lift their shoulder and pin the body with your left elbow.

3. Push your opponent's head down to create a push pull tension between the head and shoulder.

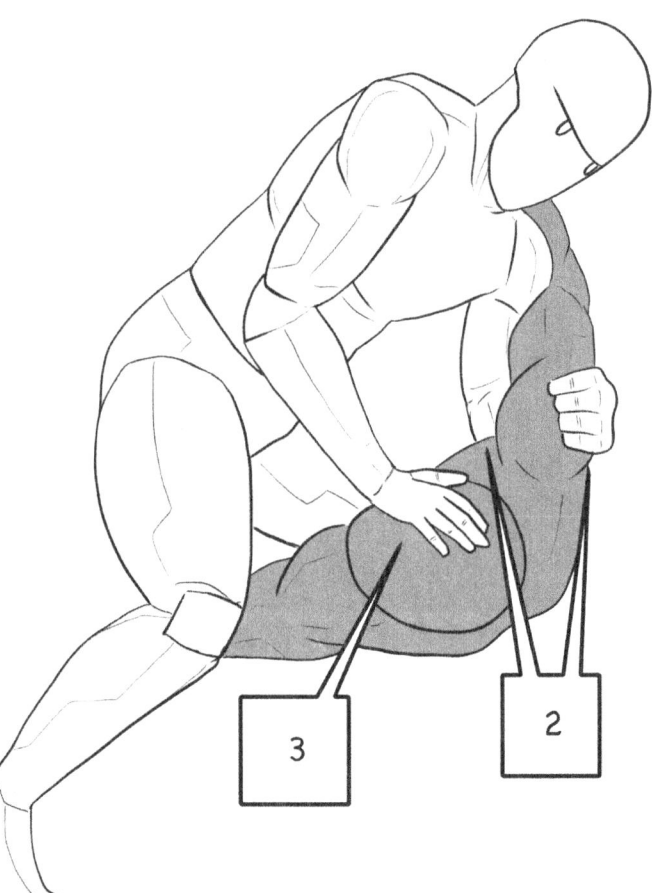

CROSS SIDE SPINNING ARMBAR

3. Spin to the other side of your opponent's body. Stay off of your knees.

4. Sit down as you pull your opponent's arm to you.

5. Bring your hips under your opponent as much as possible.

6. Bring your right leg over your opponent's torso. Bring your heels in to pull your opponent into you.

7. Hug your opponent's arm. Slowly pull back till the arm locks out.

NORTH SOUTH ARMBAR

1. Slide your wrist into the left armpit of your opponent. Pull your wrist towards you to lock your opponent's arm in place.

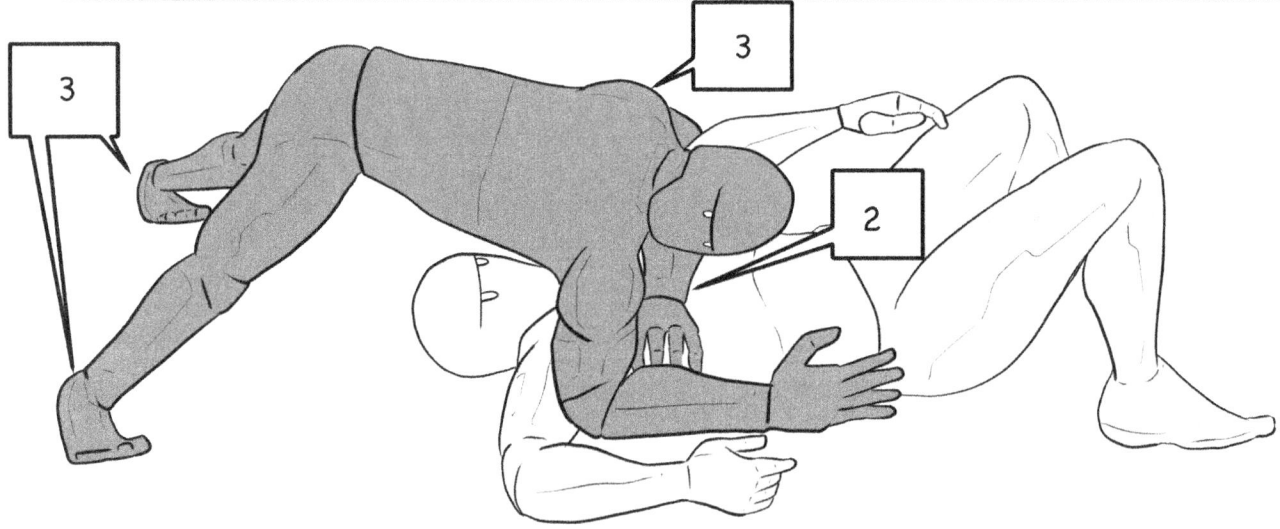

2. Slide your left forearm all the way in. Pull your forearm towards you.

3. Drive off of your toes and push your left shoulder into your opponent's left arm.

NORTH SOUTH ARMBAR

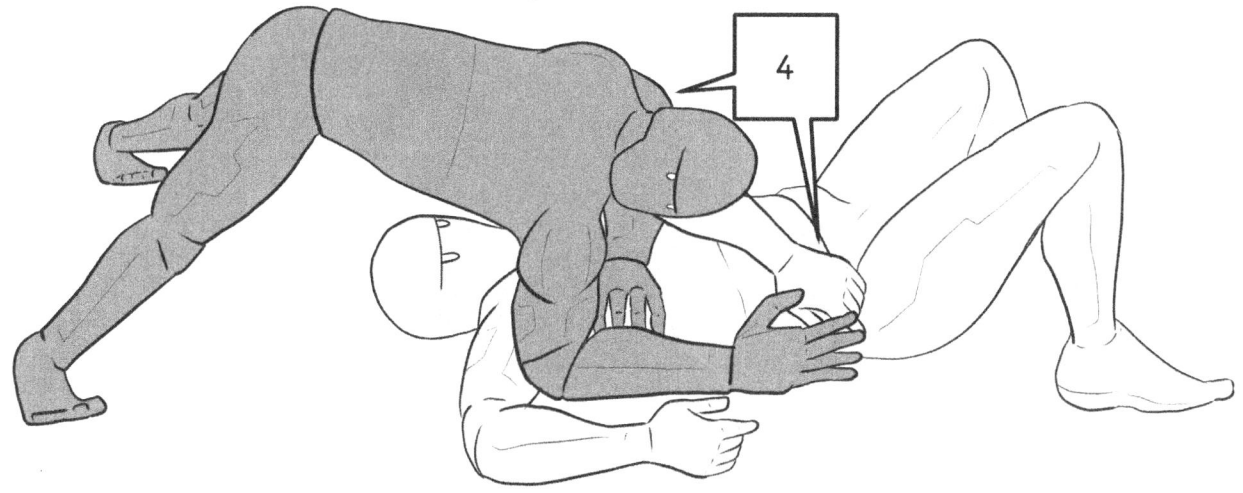

4. Drive your left shoulder towards your opponent's right hip. This will bring your opponent's left hand close to your right hand.

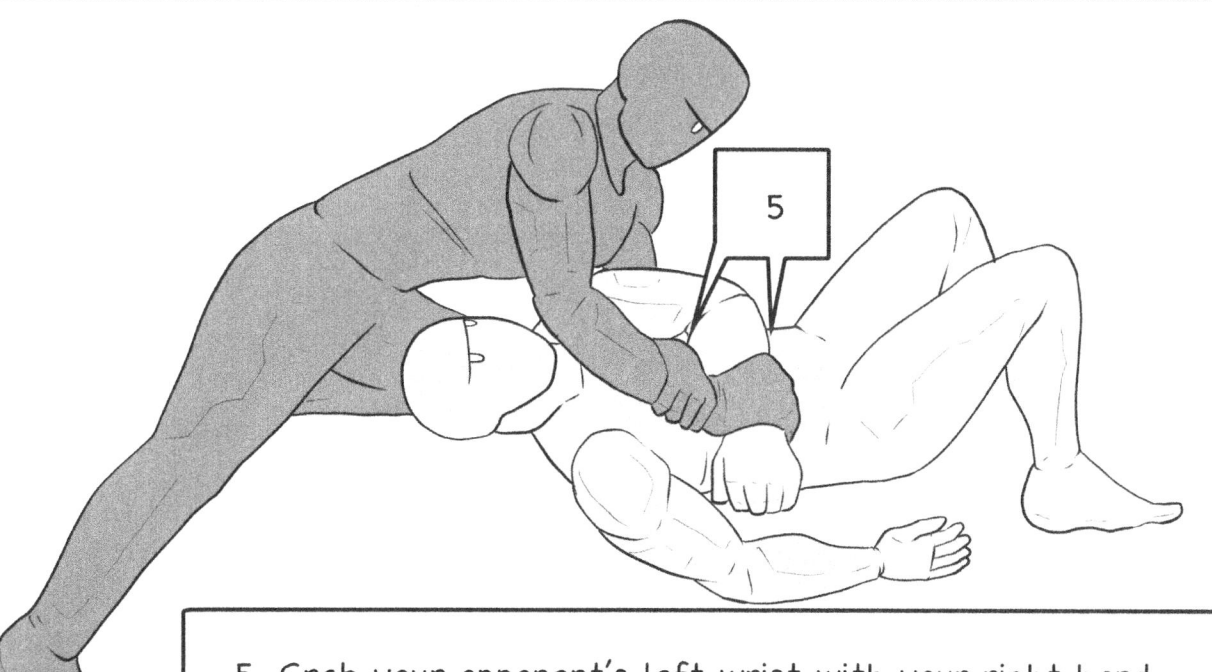

5. Grab your opponent's left wrist with your right hand. Grab your right wrist with your left hand to form the figure of four lock.

NORTH SOUTH ARMBAR

6. Use the figure four lock to turn your opponent sideways. Wedge your left knee deep into your opponent's lower back.

7. Swing your right leg over your opponent's head.

8. Sit down on your right side. Push your opponent's head down with your right thigh as you sit.

9. Shift your weight to the right to take the weight off of your left leg. You will need to do this to bring your left knee up.

10. Pinch your knees together to lock your opponent's arm in place. Hug your opponent's arm and slowly pull back till the arm locks out.

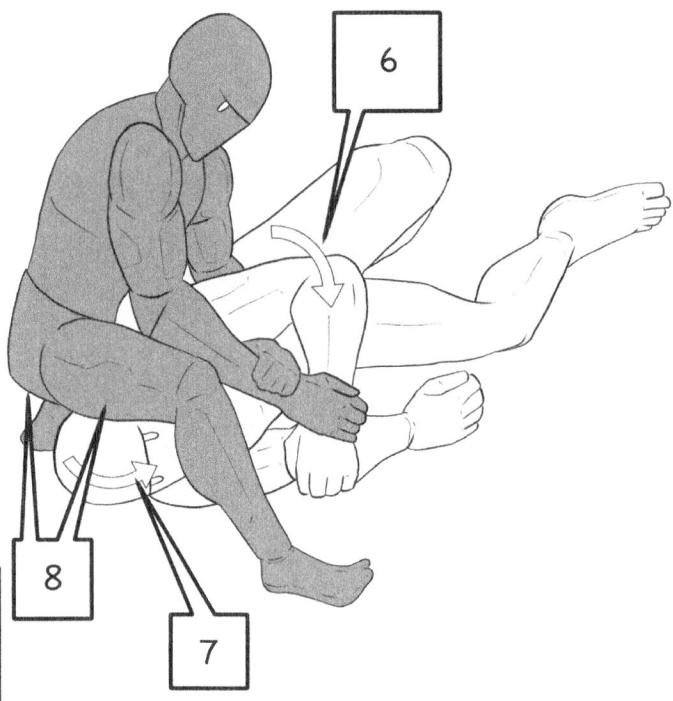
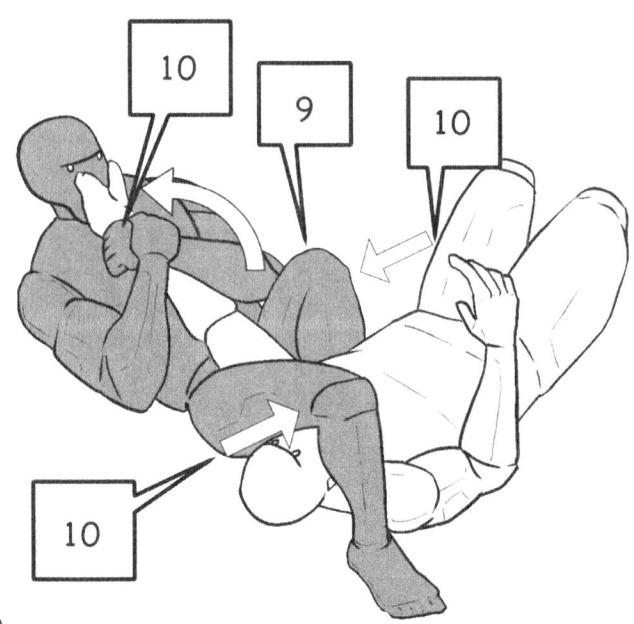

NORTH SOUTH PAPER CUTTER CHOKE

1. Set up the paper cutter choke with your left elbow in your opponent's armpit and your left hand by their hip.

2. Roll your left shoulder down, wrap your left arm around your opponent's arm.

3. Grip your opponent's collar with your left hand, palm up, four fingers in, thumb out.

4. Pivoting off the left shoulder on your opponent, spin your body to the left.

5. Keep your knees off the ground, and your legs wide.

6. Keep your right shoulder up to have space to setup your choke.

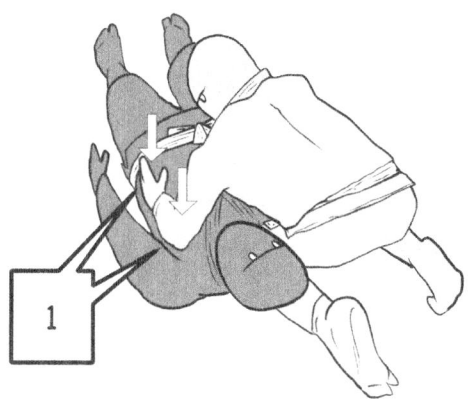
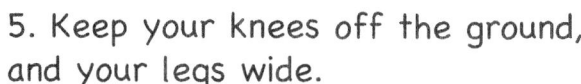
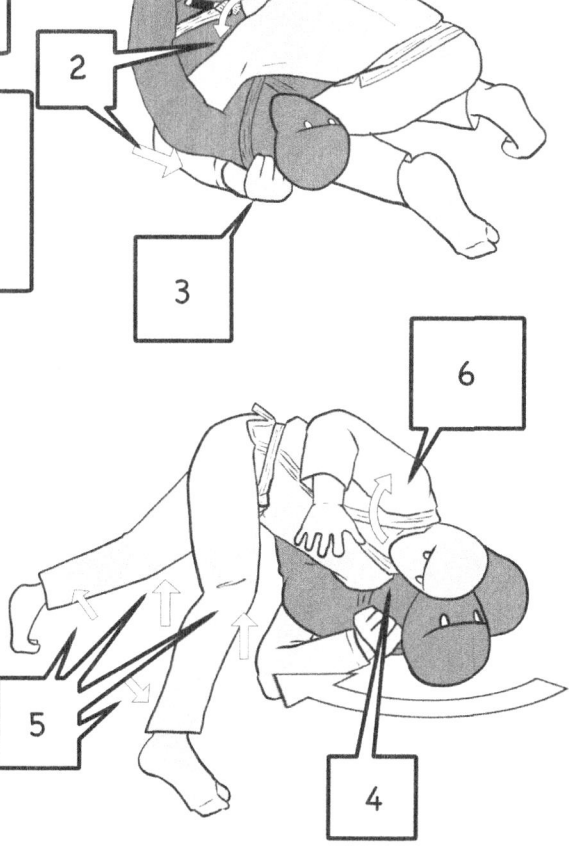

NORTH SOUTH PAPER CUTTER CHOKE

7. Slide your right hand from the left side of your opponent's neck to the right. On the right side of the neck, grab the collar with thumb in, four fingers out.

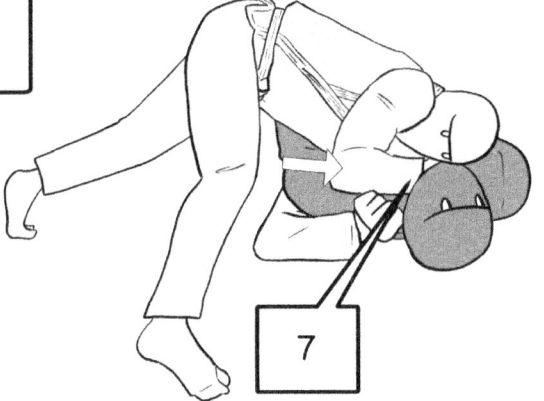

8. Slowly shift your weight from your left shoulder to your right forearm as you drop your elbow to the ground, applying the choke.

9. Sink your whole body down low. Open your elbow to your right to tighten the choke.

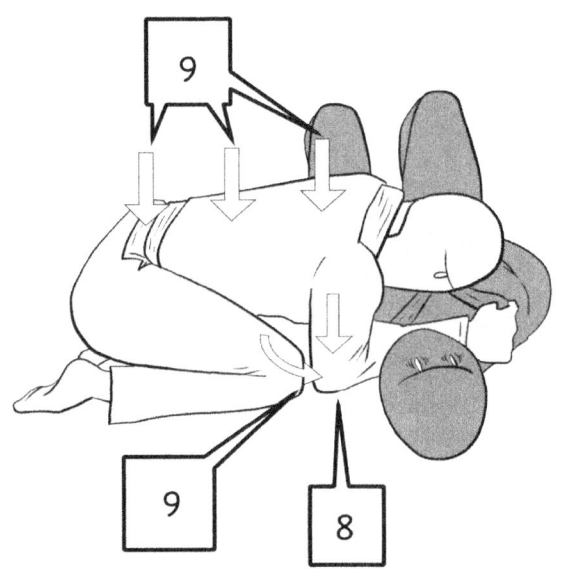

TURTLE POSITION CLOCK CHOKE

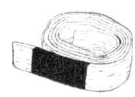 

1. Your left hand will open up your opponent's lapel on the left side. Slide your right hand under your opponent's neck, latching on to the left side of your opponent's lapel, above your left hand grip. Pull your opponent's lapel down with your left hand as your right hand slides up towards your opponent's neck. Grip tightly with your right hand.

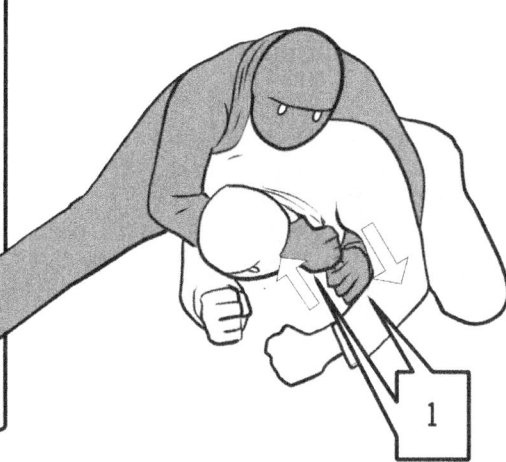

2. Release the collar grip with your left hand and grab your opponent's left wrist. Pull your opponent's wrist towards their stomach.

3. Pull your right hand back towards your right hip to start applying the choke.

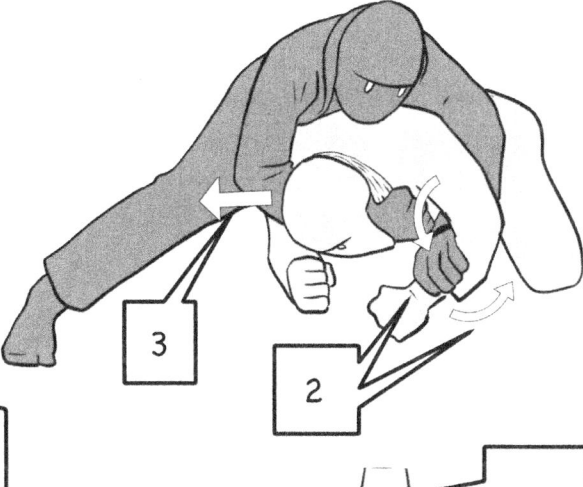

4. With your legs wide, shift your body weight over your opponent's head. Rest the left side of your body on your opponent's head to drive their head into the choke.

5. Kick your right leg out to the right. This leg will serve as a kickstand to keep you from falling off of your opponent.

OPEN GUARD TOP ANKLE LOCK

1. Grab your opponent's shins, push them forward. Assist your push with your left shin driving into your opponent's right leg.

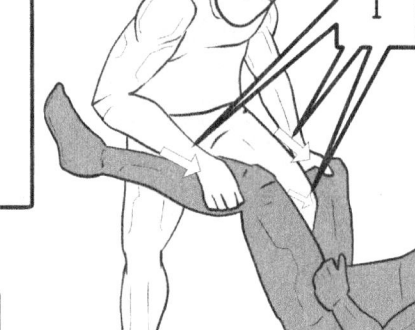

2. Wrap your right arm around your opponent's left leg. Slide back until you reach the heel.

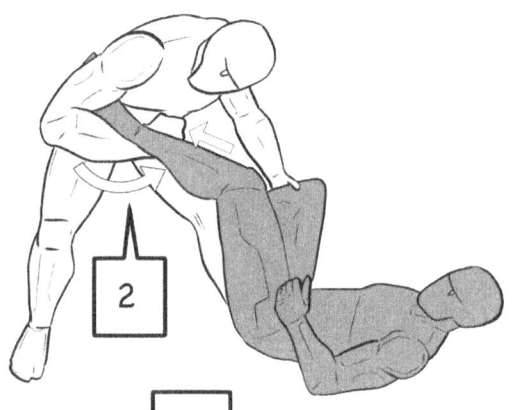

3. Hold on tight to your opponent's foot, sit down by dragging your opponent's foot back. This will slow your drop. Keep your shoulders forward and keep your ankle lock tight when you sit down.

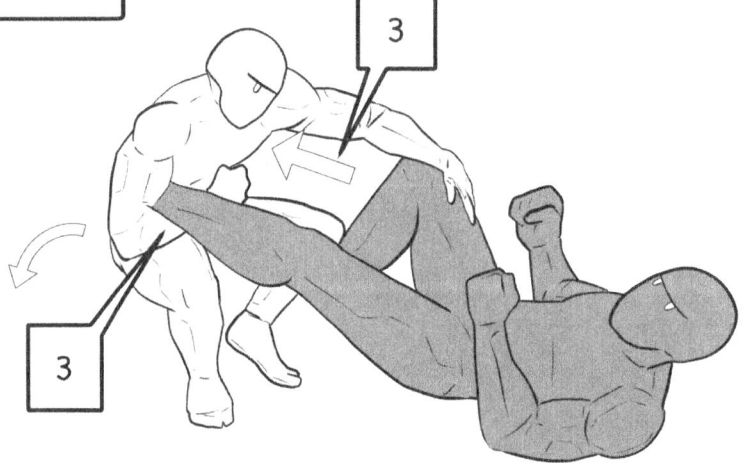

OPEN GUARD TOP ANKLE LOCK

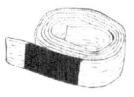 

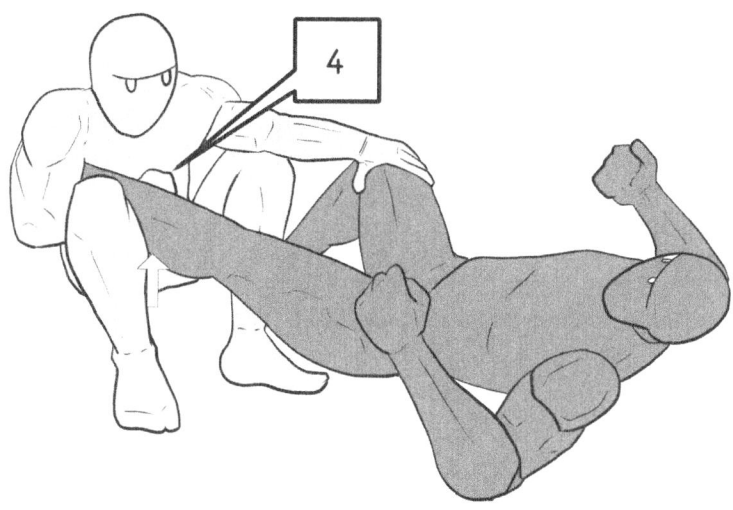

4. Drive your opponent's achilles tendon up with your wrist bone.

5. Make a fist with your right hand. Support your right fist by wrapping your left hand from the bottom.

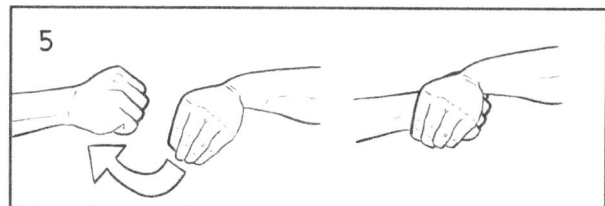

6. Pull your right fist up as high as you can with your left support hand.

7. Wrap your left foot around your opponent's left leg.

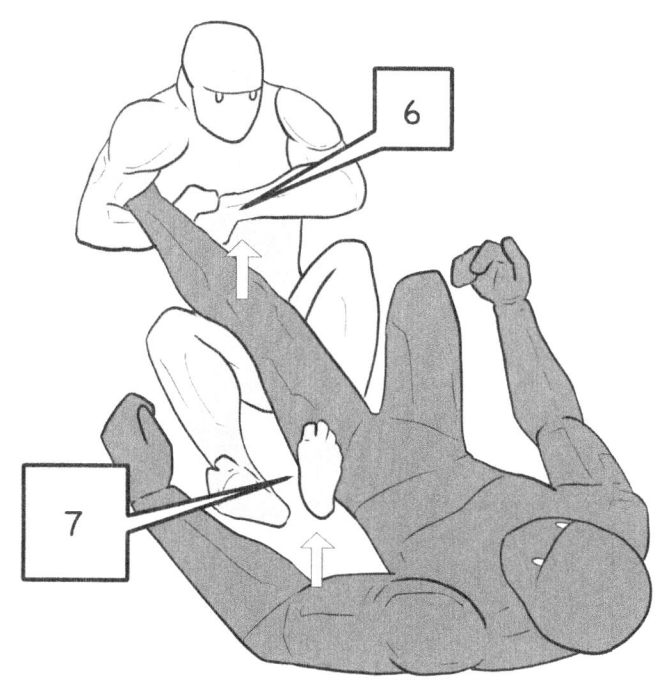

OPEN GUARD TOP ANKLE LOCK

8. Place the right foot on your opponent's hip, heel up, toes down.

9. Drop down on your right elbow. Pinch your knees together.

10. Slowly pull up your wrist bone into your opponent's achilles tendon, drive your hips forward and swing your shoulders back until the ankle locks out.

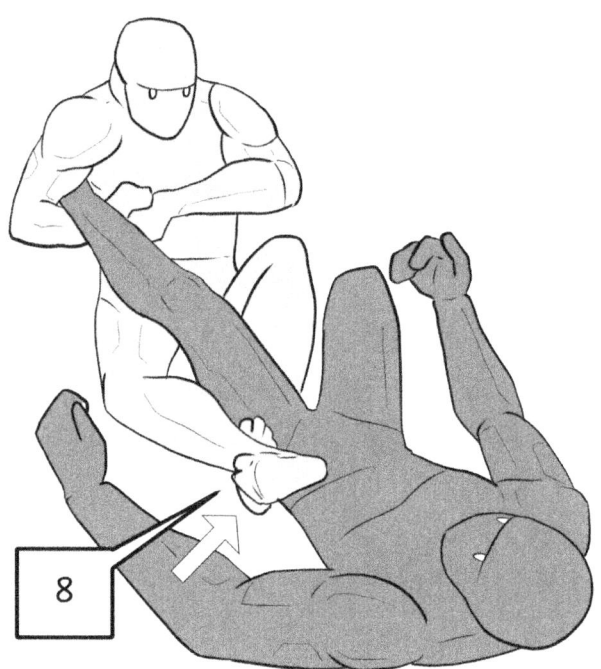

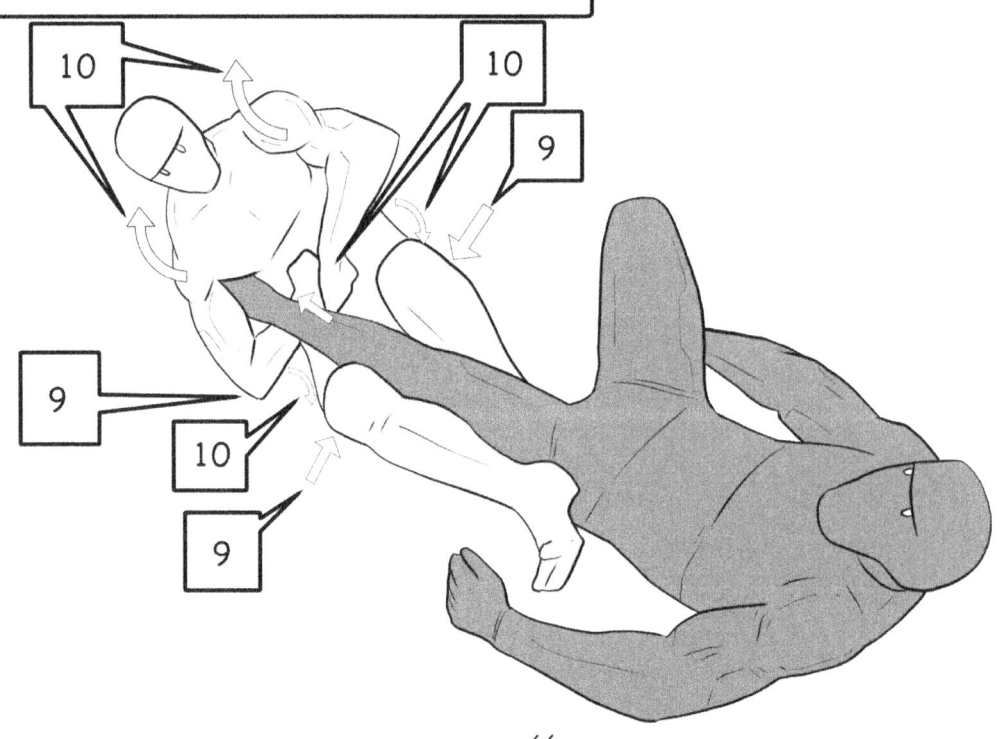

GUARD BOTTOM ARMBAR

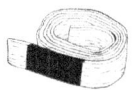 

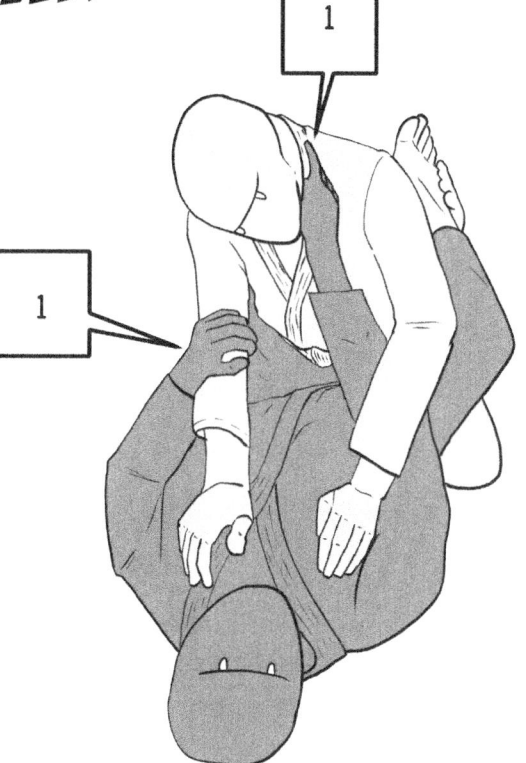

1. Grip your opponent's collar with your right hand. Grip your opponent's arm with your left hand.

2. Place the ball of your left foot on your opponent's right hip.

3. Push the inside of your left knee into your opponent.

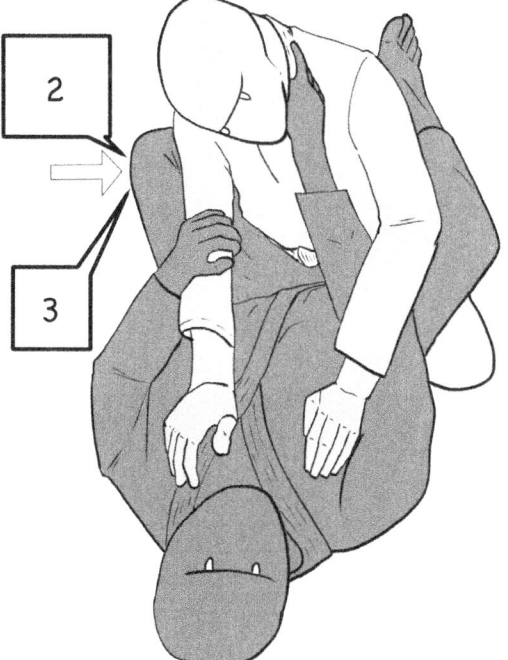

GUARD BOTTOM ARMBAR

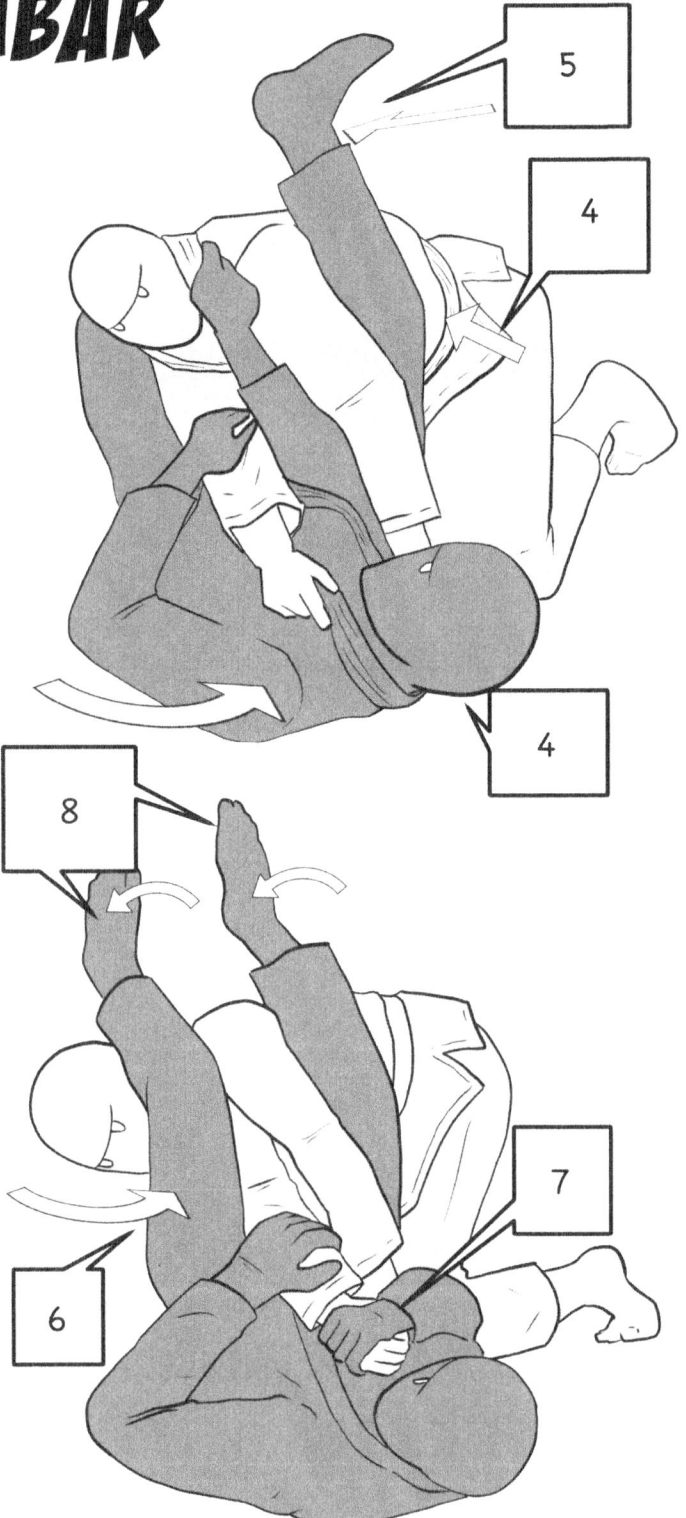

4. Push off of your left foot and swing your right shoulder by your opponent's left knee. Simultaneously, swing your right leg deep into your opponent's armpit.

5. Drive your opponent's torso down with your right leg. This will keep your opponent off balance.

6. Swing your left leg over your opponent's head.

7. Release collar with your right hand and grab your opponent's hand and attach it to the middle of your chest. Point your opponent's right thumb up.

8. Drive your heels down, left heel pushing your opponent's head down, right heel pushing your opponent's torso down. Drive your hips up slowly till your opponent's elbow locks out.

GUARD BOTTOM KIMURA

1. Bring your hands to the inside of your opponent's arms.

2. Drive your hips up.

3. Drive your opponent's arms out and down to the ground by shooting your hands up and circling them to the outside.

4. Grab your opponent's left wrist with your right hand. Open your guard, drive off of your left foot to sit up, wrap your left arm over your opponent's left arm and grab your wrist to catch the kimura lock.

GUARD BOTTOM KIMURA

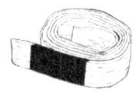 

5. Close your guard, bring your back to the ground and drive your opponent down to your left

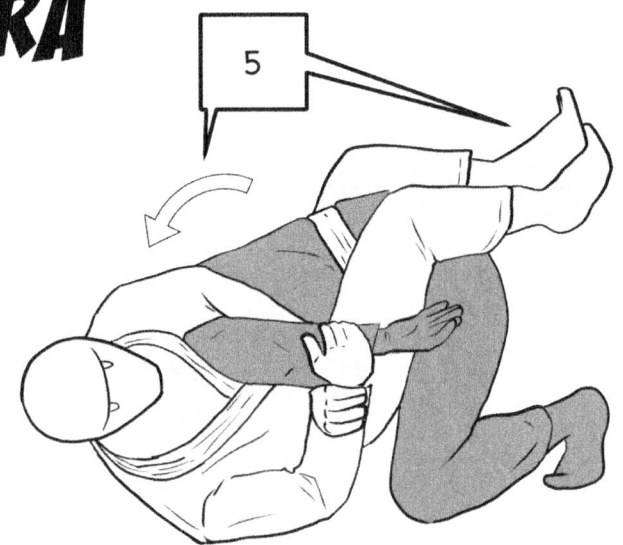

6. Plant your right toes into the ground, drive off of your right toes to turn towards your opponent.

7. Lock your guard.

8. Bring your left elbow down, push your opponent's left wrist up over their left shoulder slowly until their shoulder locks out.

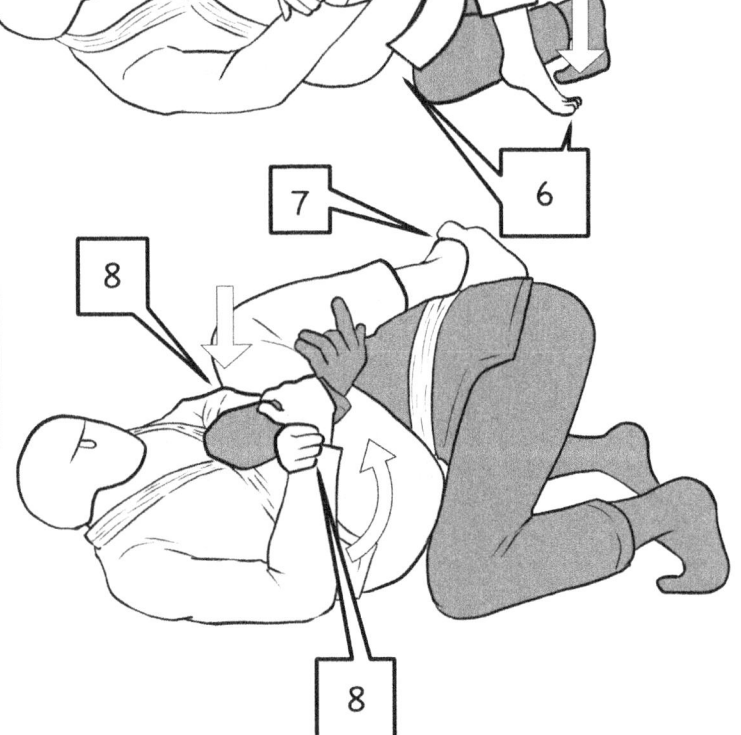

GUARD BOTTOM CROSS CHOKE

1. Open your opponent's left side lapel with your right hand. Grip your opponent's left side lapel behind your opponent's neck with your left hand, four fingers in, thumb out.

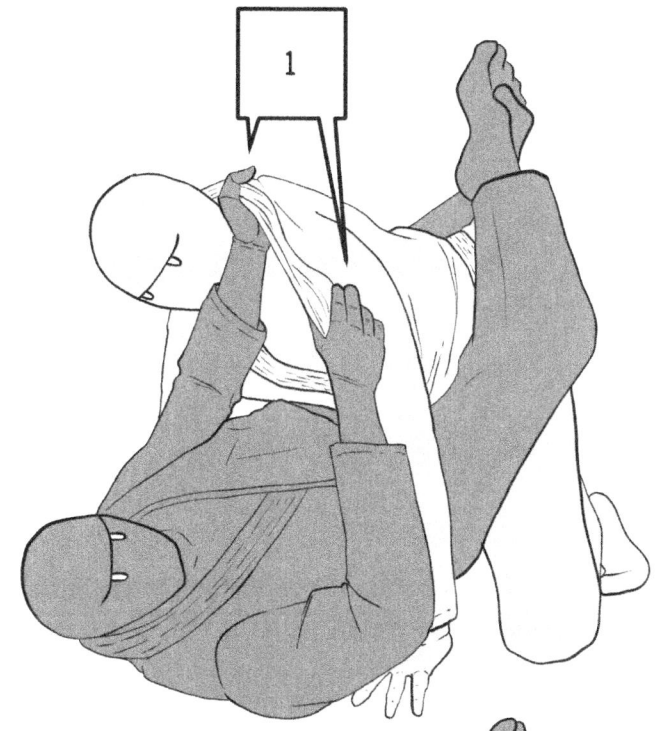

2. Slide your body to the right side, creating space for your right hand to go under your left arm and grip your opponent's right side lapel.

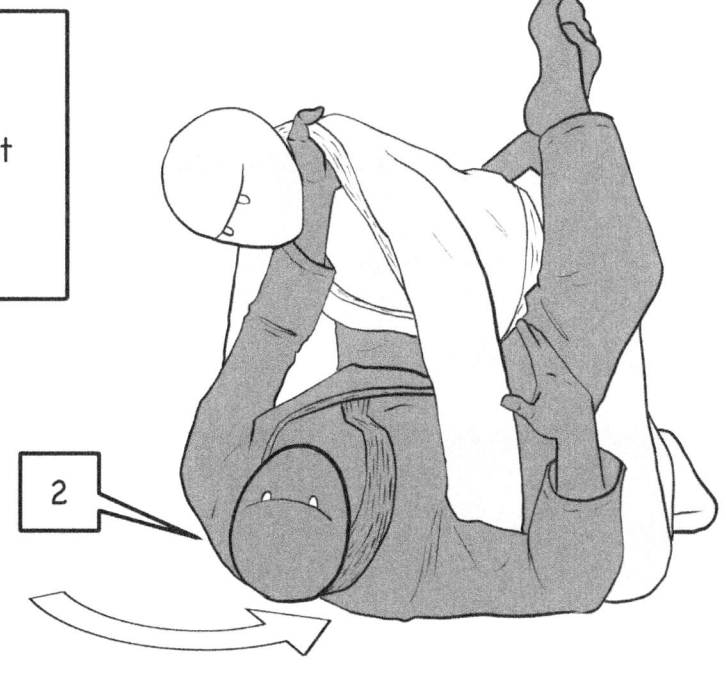

GUARD BOTTOM CROSS CHOKE

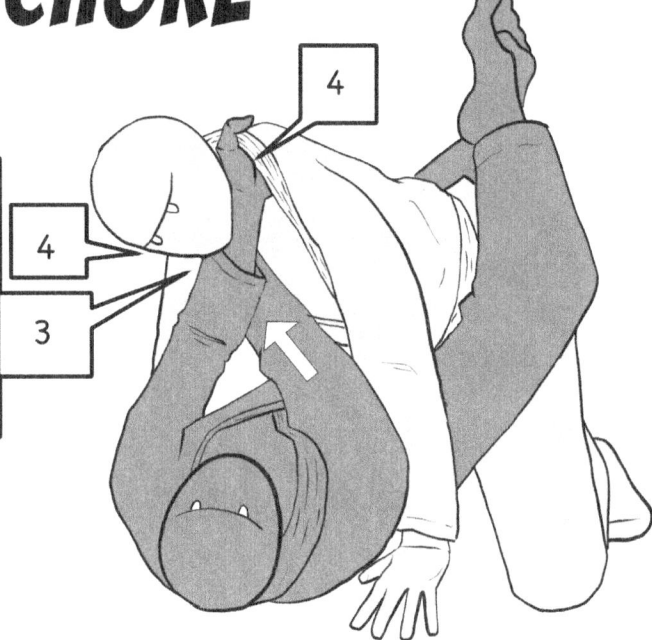

3. Slide your right hand under your left arm and grip the collar as deep as possible, four fingers in, thumb out.

4. Push your wrists in to the side of your opponent's neck.

5. Pull your opponent down and drag your elbows down on your ribs.

6. Connect your head next to your opponent's head. This will make it difficult for your opponent to create space for escape.

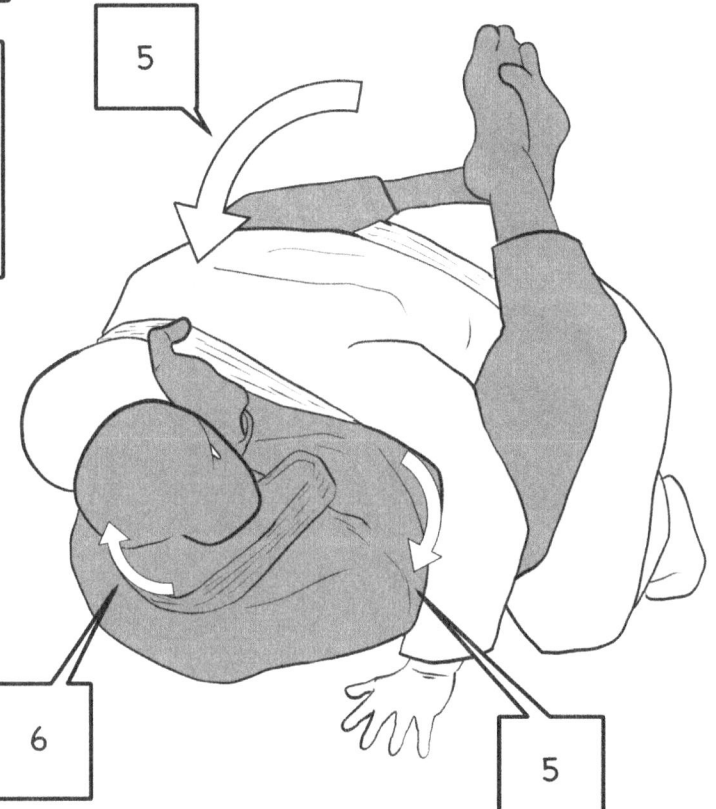

HOW TO BUILD YOUR GAME

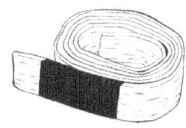

- GAME PLAN
- HOW TO PRACTICE TECHNIQUES
- THINGS TO KEEP IN MIND DURING ROLLS

GUARD TOP GAME PLAN

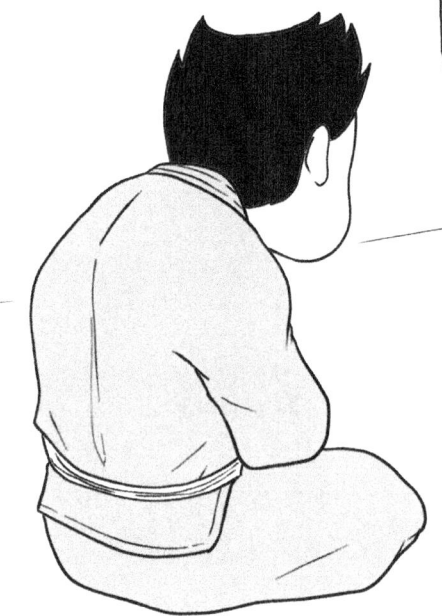

RYAN KIMURA
3 STRIPE WHITEBELT

VS

I'M NOT GONNA LOSE TO ANOTHER WHITE BELT!

JAMES GARCIA
FIRST DAY OF JIU JITSU

SLAP!

BUMP!

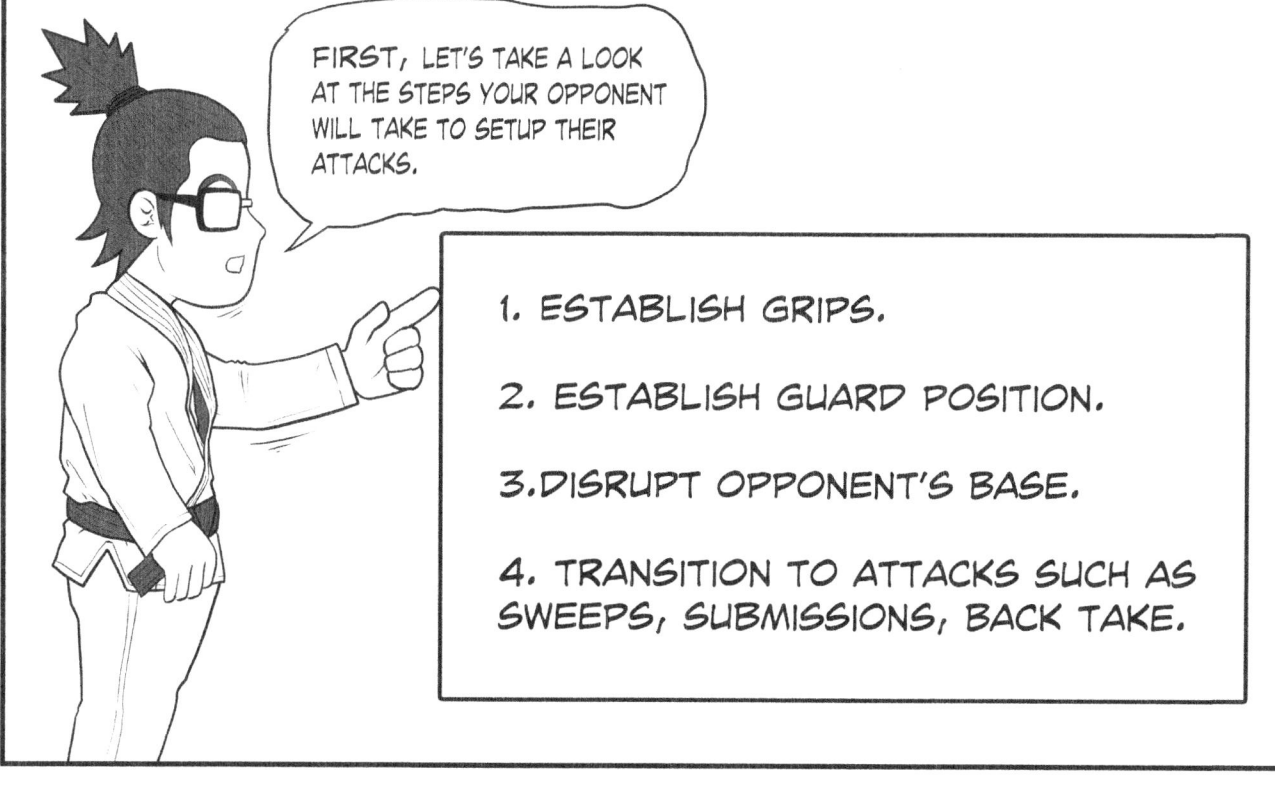

WE WILL VISIT THE STEPS YOU NEED TO TAKE IN ORDER TO INITIATE YOUR OFFENSE VERY SOON. FIRST WE HAVE TO MAKE SURE YOU CAN STAY IN GUARD TOP LONG ENOUGH TO START YOUR OFFENSE.

YOUR FIRST GOAL WHEN STARTING FROM TOP POSITION IN A JIU JITSU ROLL, IS TO STAY ON TOP.

LET'S TAKE A LOOK AT THE ROLL BETWEEN JAMES AND RYAN TO SEE WHERE IT WENT WRONG!

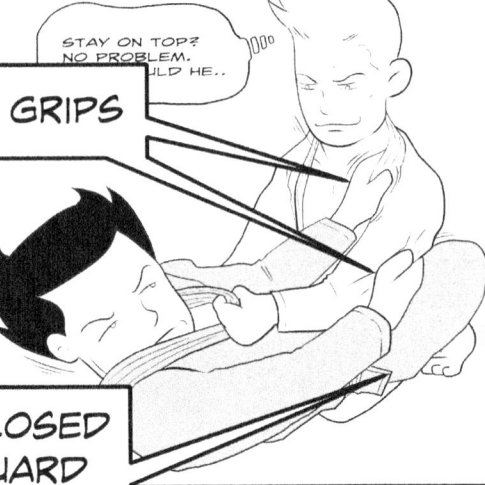

STAY ON TOP? NO PROBLEM. WOULD HE..

GRIPS

CLOSED GUARD

AS YOU CAN SEE ON THE TOP FRAME, RYAN ALREADY HAS GRIPS AND GUARD ESTABLISHED.

RYAN IS ALREADY 2 STEPS AHEAD OF JAMES.

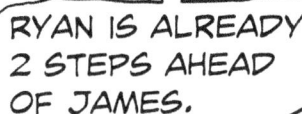

WEIGHT SHIFT FORWARD

ON THE BOTTOM FRAME, RYAN IS OFF BALANCING JAMES BY SHIFTING HIS WEIGHT FORWARD, ELONGATING HIS LEFT ARM WHICH STARTS TO MAKE RYAN FALL TO THE LEFT. RYAN IS ALSO BLOCKING AND PUSHING RYAN'S LEFT LEG WITH HIS RIGHT LEG TO TRIP HIM UP.

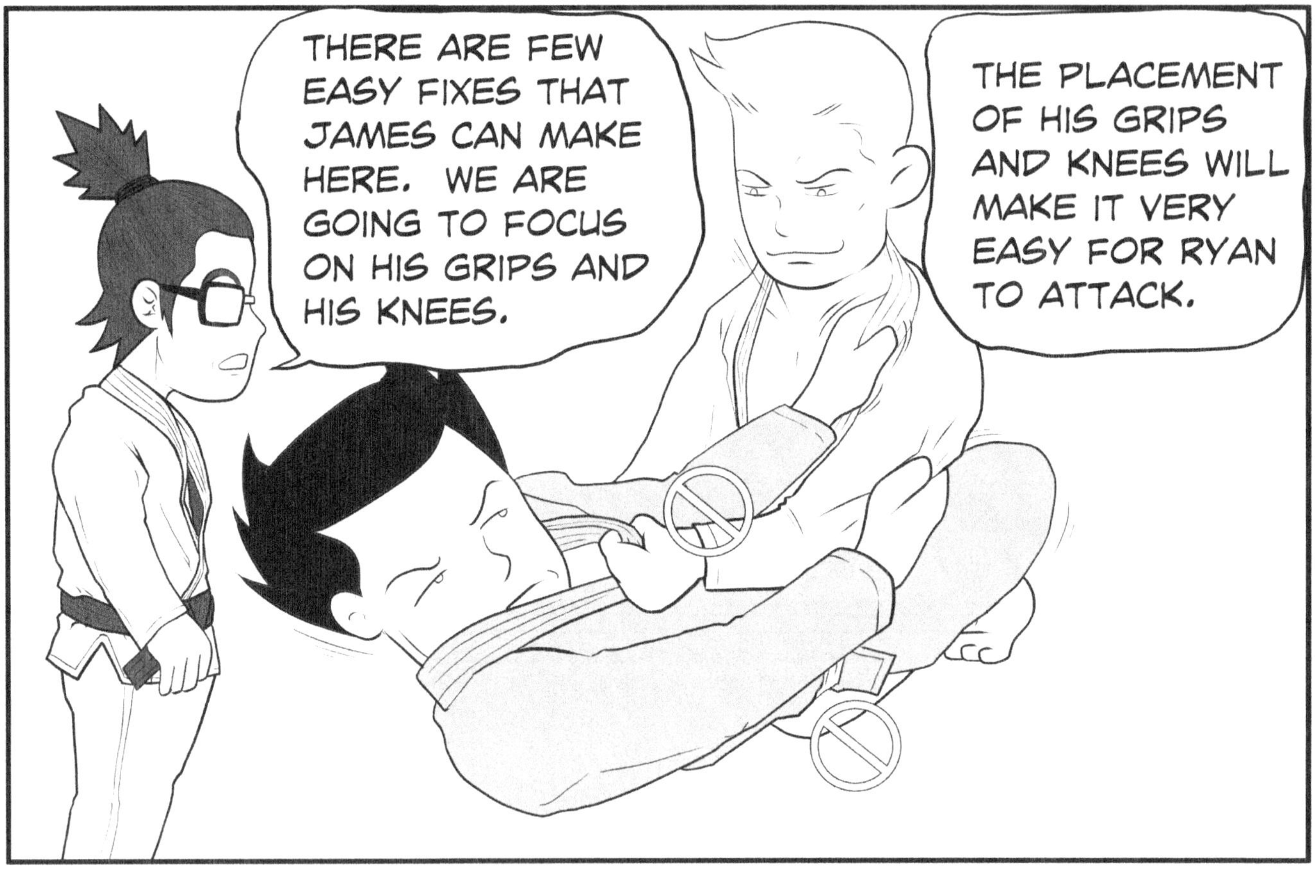

THERE ARE FEW EASY FIXES THAT JAMES CAN MAKE HERE. WE ARE GOING TO FOCUS ON HIS GRIPS AND HIS KNEES.

THE PLACEMENT OF HIS GRIPS AND KNEES WILL MAKE IT VERY EASY FOR RYAN TO ATTACK.

HERE, RYAN HAS HIS BODY TURNED TO THE RIGHT AND HAS A GRIP ON JAMES' LEFT ARM. THIS MEANS THAT RYAN WILL MOST LIKELY ATTEMPT A SWEEP TO THE RIGHT OR ATTACK JAMES' LEFT ARM.

RYAN CAN ALSO COLLAR DRAG JAMES TO HIS LEFT OR SETUP A CROSS COLLAR CHOKE.

DOUBLE BELT GRIP FROM GUARD TOP IS ONE OF THE BEST WAYS TO KEEP YOURSELF SAFE FROM SWEEPS AND SUBMISSIONS. IT KEEPS YOUR OPPONENT'S HIPS GROUNDED, MAKING IT VERY DIFFICULT TO INITIATE OFFENSE.

DRIVE YOUR HIPS BACK TOWARDS YOUR OPPONENT'S ANKLES AS YOU DRIVE YOUR BELT GRIP FORWARD TO BREAK OPEN YOUR OPPONENT'S GUARD.

IT IS VERY DIFFICULT FOR YOUR OPPONENT TO BREAK THIS GRIP. USE YOUR PALMS THROUGH YOUR GRIPS TO PUSH YOUR OPPONENT DOWN AND AWAY.

KEEP YOUR KNEES WIDE FOR EXTRA STABILITY. BE READY TO USE YOUR KNEE AS A KICKSTAND WHEN YOUR OPPONENT TRIES TO OFF BALANCE YOU.

WITH THE DOUBLE BELT GRIP, YOUR HEAD POSITION IS NOT MUCH OF A CONCERN, BUT IT IS IMPORTANT TO NOTE, THAT IN GENERAL, YOU SHOULD KEEP YOUR HEAD UP IN GUARD TOP. WHEN YOU TILT YOUR HEAD DOWN, YOUR POSTURE WILL SUFFER, MAKING IT EASIER FOR YOUR OPPONENT TO BREAKDOWN YOUR BASE.

YOUR POSTURE IS AT IT'S STRONGEST WHEN YOUR ELBOWS ARE UNDER YOUR SHOULDERS. ROLL YOUR SHOULDERS FORWARD AND KEEP YOUR ELBOWS IN, UNLESS YOU NEED TO PUSH OR PULL YOUR OPPONENT. WHEN YOUR ARMS ARE NOT IN USE, BRING IT BACK UNDER YOUR SHOULDERS.

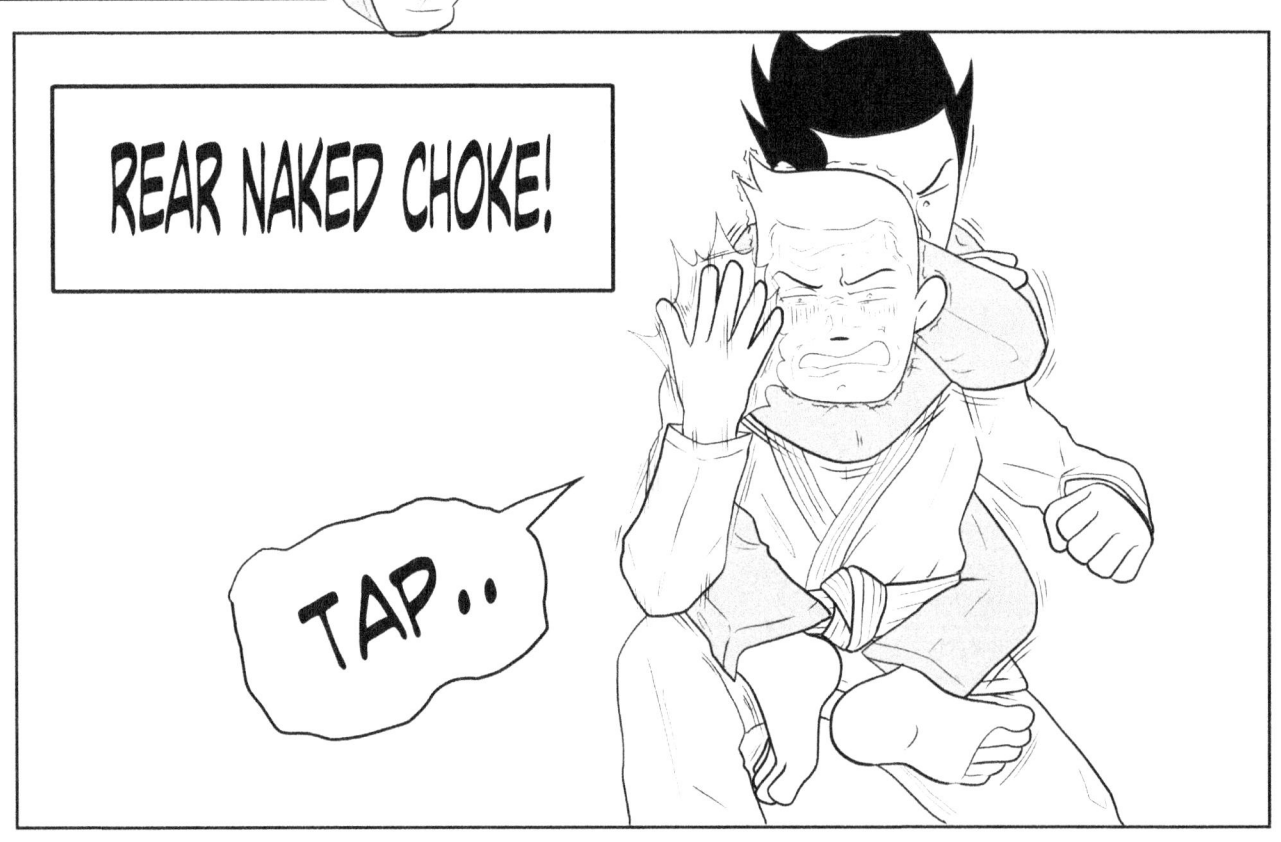

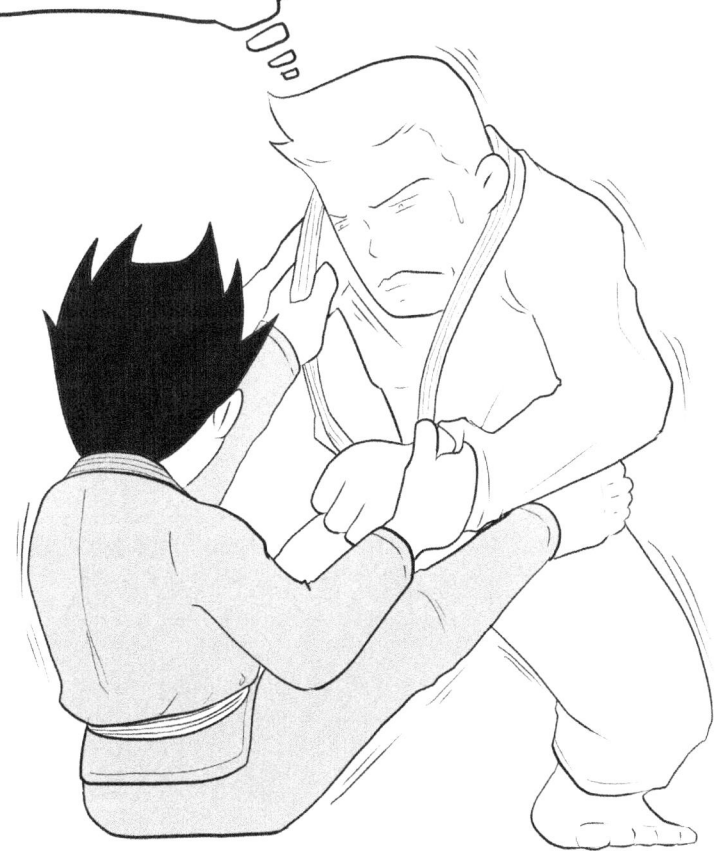

There are many guard pass options from this position. Let's look at a basic pass setup that will make it difficult for your opponent to set up their offense and makes it easier to set up your passes.

First, grab your opponent's lower legs, preferably with a gi grip.

Push your opponent's legs forward, driving their knees to their chest. Push from your toes and lean into your hands. This will nullify the use of their legs for a moment.

When your opponent fights back against the push and pushes back, go with the push of your opponent and drive your opponent's legs down to the mat. If you were unable to push your opponent's legs forward in the first place, just push the legs down.

This push pull action will make it very difficult for your opponent to set up their guard.

LET'S DO A BASIC BREAKDOWN OF ONE OF THE MOST EFFECTIVE GUARD PASS, TOREANDO PASS.

KEEP PINNING YOUR OPPONENT'S LEGS DOWN TO THE GROUND AND SPIN TO ONE SIDE OR THE OTHER.

1. KEEP YOUR ARMS FULLY EXTENDED.
2. KEEP YOUR BACK STRAIGHT.
3. LEGS WIDE TO PROVIDE STABILITY.
4. KEEP YOUR KNEES OFF THE MAT.

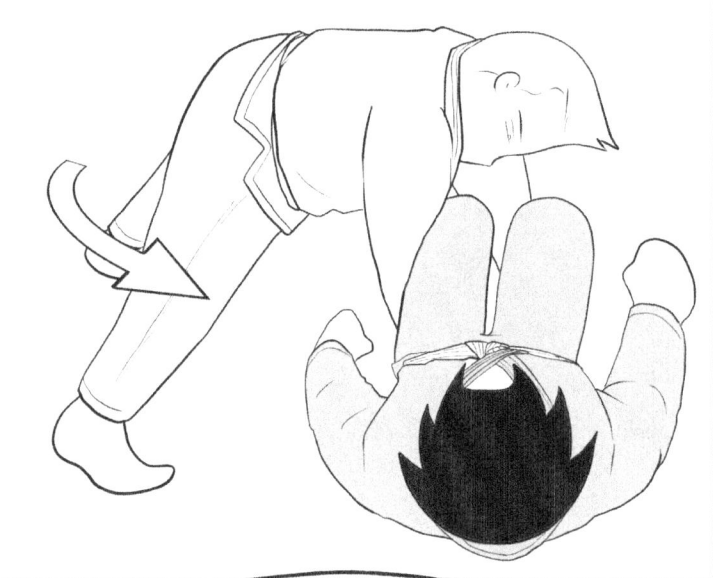

TO PIN YOUR OPPONENT, DRIVE YOUR SHOULDER DOWN TO YOUR OPPONENT'S STOMACH. KEEP YOUR BACK STRAIGHT, LEGS WIDE. DRIVE YOUR TOES INTO THE MAT AND TRANSFER THE FORWARD PRESSURE TO YOUR SHOULDER PINNING YOUR OPPONENT.

TOREANDO PASS!

3RD GOAL: HOLD ADVANTAGE POSITIONS!

CONTROL POINTS AFTER PASSING GUARD

AFTER PASSING GUARD, YOU WILL NEED TO ESTABLISH CONTROL POINTS ON YOUR OPPONENT.

YOU SHOULD LOOK TO ESTABLISH 2-3 POINTS EVERY TIME YOU LOCK DOWN A POSITION.

SHOULDER LINE

HIP LINE

EXAMPLE: CROSS SIDE WITH HEAD AND ARM

EXAMPLE: KNEE RIDE

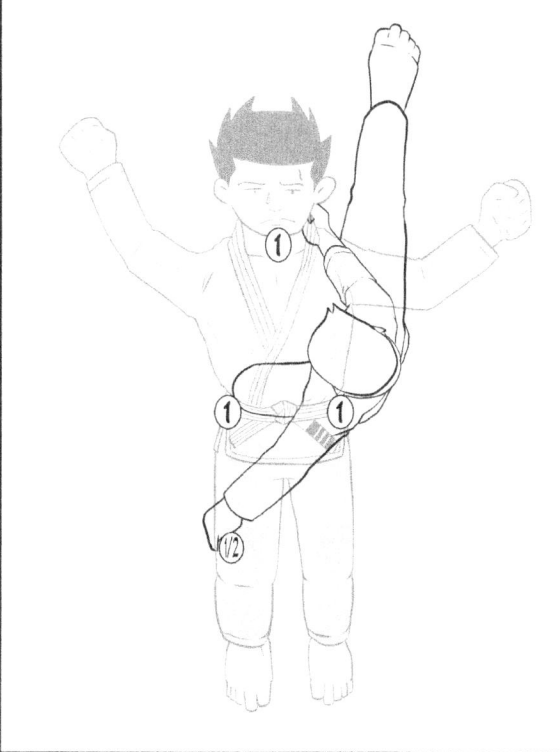

GUARD BOTTOM
GAME PLAN

1ST GOAL: GRIP AND CLOSED GUARD!

EASIEST WAY TO GET TO CLOSED GUARD IS FROM COMBAT BASE. A SITTING POSITION WITH ONE KNEE UP AND ONE KNEE DOWN.

GRAB YOUR OPPONENT'S COLLAR ON THE SAME SIDE THAT YOU HAVE THE KNEE UP.

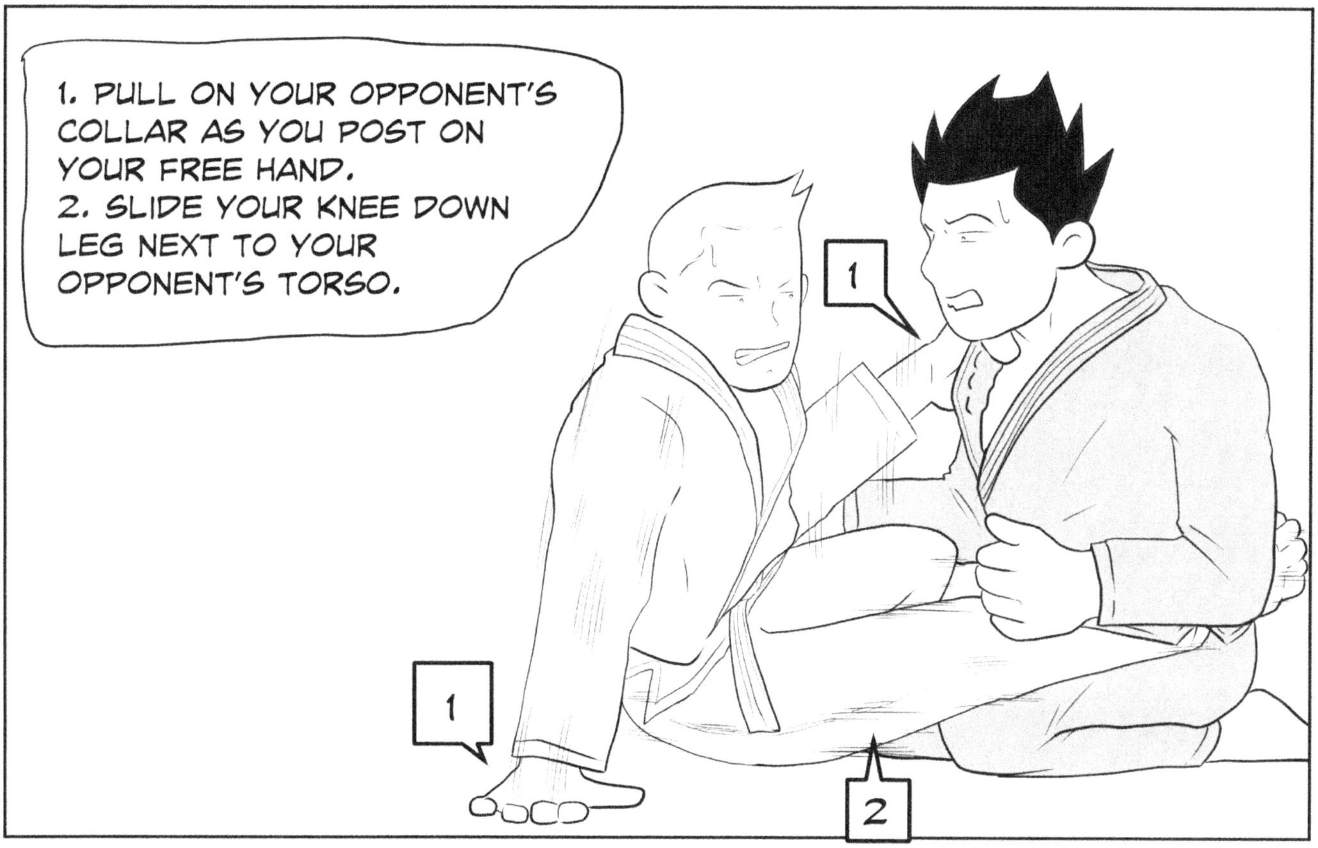

1. PULL ON YOUR OPPONENT'S COLLAR AS YOU POST ON YOUR FREE HAND.
2. SLIDE YOUR KNEE DOWN LEG NEXT TO YOUR OPPONENT'S TORSO.

3. KEEP CONSTANT PULL WITH YOUR GRIPS.
4. HOOK THE SLIDING LEG AROUND YOUR OPPONENT'S TORSO.
5. SLIDE YOUR KNEE UP LEG AROUND YOUR OPPONENT'S TORSO.
6. INTERTWINE YOUR ANKLES TO LOCK YOUR OPPONENT IN YOUR CLOSED GUARD.

2ND GOAL: SOLIDIFY CLOSED GUARD!

ONCE YOU HAVE ESTABLISHED THE CLOSED GUARD, SWITCH YOUR COLLAR GRIP TO THE CROSS COLLAR GRIP. SAME SIDE COLLAR GRIPS ARE GREAT FOR PUSHING YOUR OPPONENT AWAY, CROSS GRIPS ARE GREAT FOR PULLING YOUR OPPONENT TO YOU, WHICH MAKES FOR A GREAT OFFENSIVE GRIP TO SET UP YOUR SWEEPS, SUBMISSIONS AND BACK TAKES.

NEXT, IMPROVE THE SLEEVE GRIP BY GRIPPING BEHIND THE TRICEPS. THIS WILL MAKE IT HARDER FOR YOUR OPPONENT TO BREAK YOUR GRIP AND WILL REQUIRE LESS EFFORT TO PULL YOUR OPPONENT FORWARD.

YOUR COLLAR GRIP SHOULD BE ON THE INSIDE OF YOUR OPPONENT'S ARMS. THIS INSIDE POSITION WILL MAKE IT DIFFICULT FOR YOUR OPPONENT TO PUSH YOU AWAY. YOUR SLEEVE GRIP SHOULD BE ON THE OUTSIDE OF YOUR OPPONENT'S ARM. THIS WILL MAKE IT DIFFICULT FOR YOUR OPPONENT TO POST THEIR ARM OUT DURING YOUR SWEEP ATTEMPTS.

TRICEPS GI GRIP

THE KEY TO A GOOD GUARD IS TO KEEP DISRUPTING YOUR OPPONENT'S BASE SO IT IS DIFFICULT FOR THEM TO START THEIR MOVE. HERE JAMES IS PULLING RYAN DOWN USING THE CROSS COLLAR GRIP, SLEEVE GRIP AND HIS LEGS.

3RD GOAL: SETUP YOUR OFFENSE!

IN PRACTICE ROLLS, YOU WON'T FIND TOO MANY PEOPLE ACTIVELY SEEKING OUT CLOSED GUARD DUE TO THE STAGNANT NATURE OF THE GUARD. HOWEVER, IN COMPETITION YOU WILL SEE CLOSED GUARD OFTEN. I BELIEVE CLOSED GUARD IS THE FIRST GUARD YOU SHOULD LEARN FOR MANY REASONS, THE BIGGEST ONE BEING THAT YOU GET TO SLOW DOWN THE ROLL AND GIVE YOURSELF TIME TO THINK AND PLAN OUT YOUR ATTACK. IT DOESN'T HURT THAT MOST OF YOUR OPPONENT'S ATTACK OPTIONS WILL BE NULLIFIED TILL THEY OPEN YOUR CLOSED GUARD.

LET'S LOOK AT ONE OF THE MOST BEGINNER FRIENDLY SWEEPS AVAILABLE FROM THE CLOSED GUARD, THE SCISSOR SWEEP.

TURN TO YOUR SLEEVE GRIP SIDE.
1. SLIDE THE TOP KNEE BELOW YOUR OPPONENT'S SHOULDER.
2. PULL YOUR OPPONENT FORWARD AND TO YOUR SLEEVE GRIP SIDE WITH YOUR GRIPS AND WITH YOUR TOP LEG.
3. ONCE YOUR OPPONENT'S WEIGHT HAS SHIFTED, DROP YOUR BOTTOM LEG DOWN BY THE SIDE OF YOUR OPPONENT'S LEG.

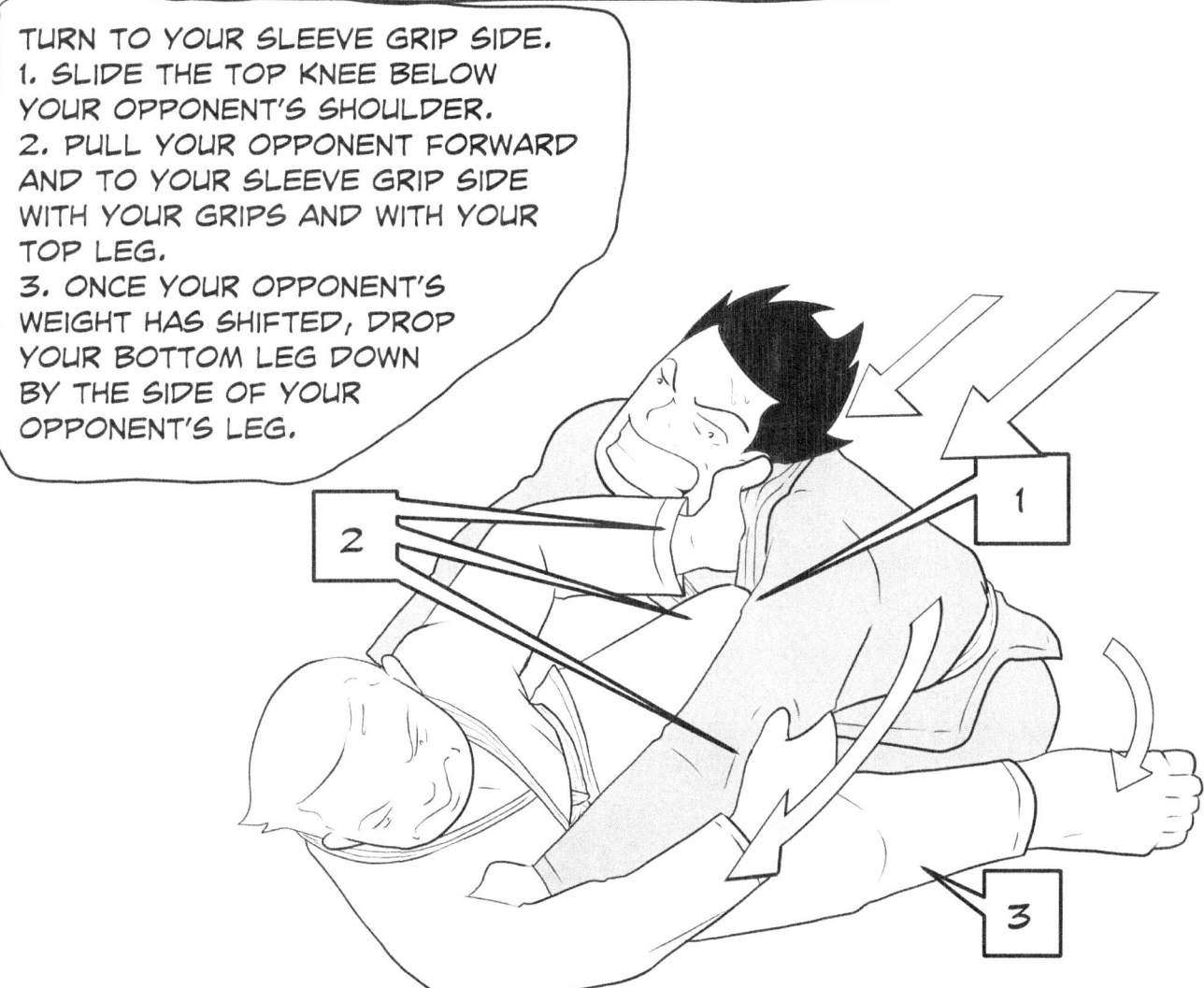

4. LIFT YOUR ELBOW UP TO TURN OVER YOUR OPPONENT'S HEAD.
5. KICK YOUR LEGS IN A SCISSOR MOTION, TOP LEG KICKING YOUR OPPONENT OVER YOUR BOTTOM LEG AND YOUR BOTTOM LEG CHOPPING IN YOUR OPPONENT'S LEGS.
6. LOOK IN THE DIRECTION THAT YOU WANT TO TAKE YOUR OPPONENT.

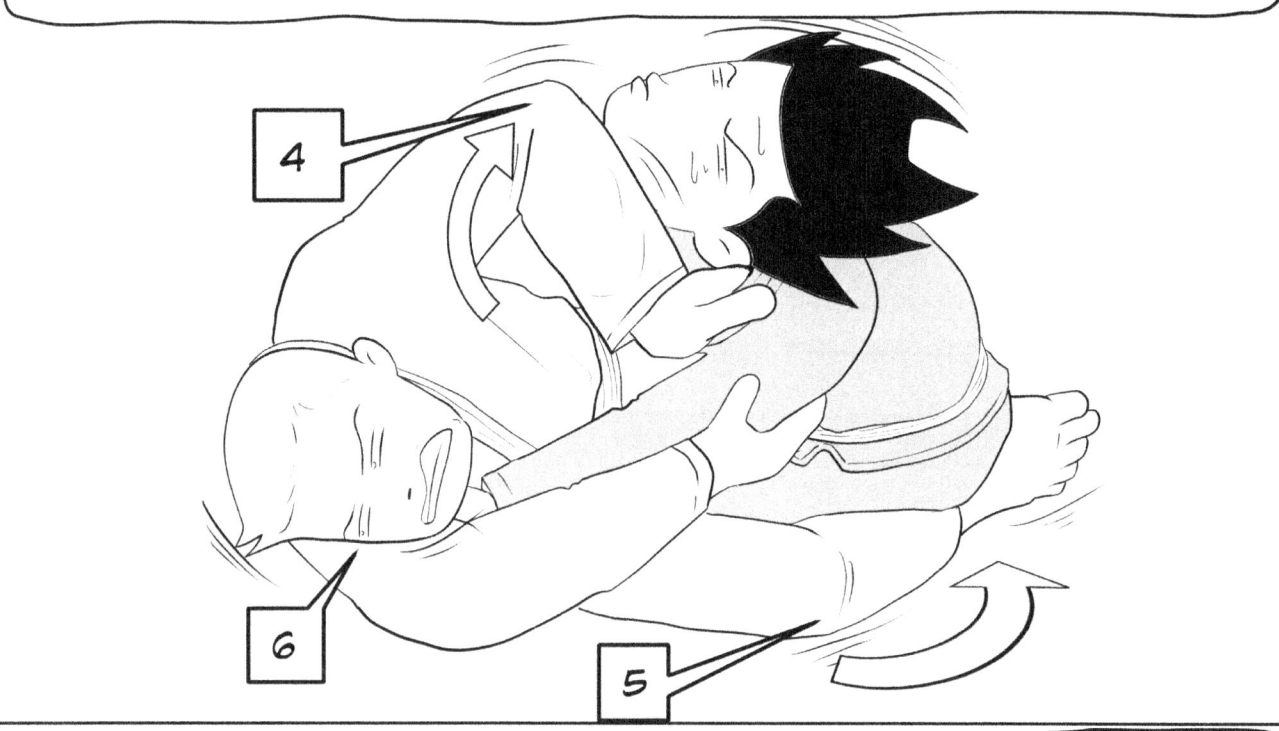

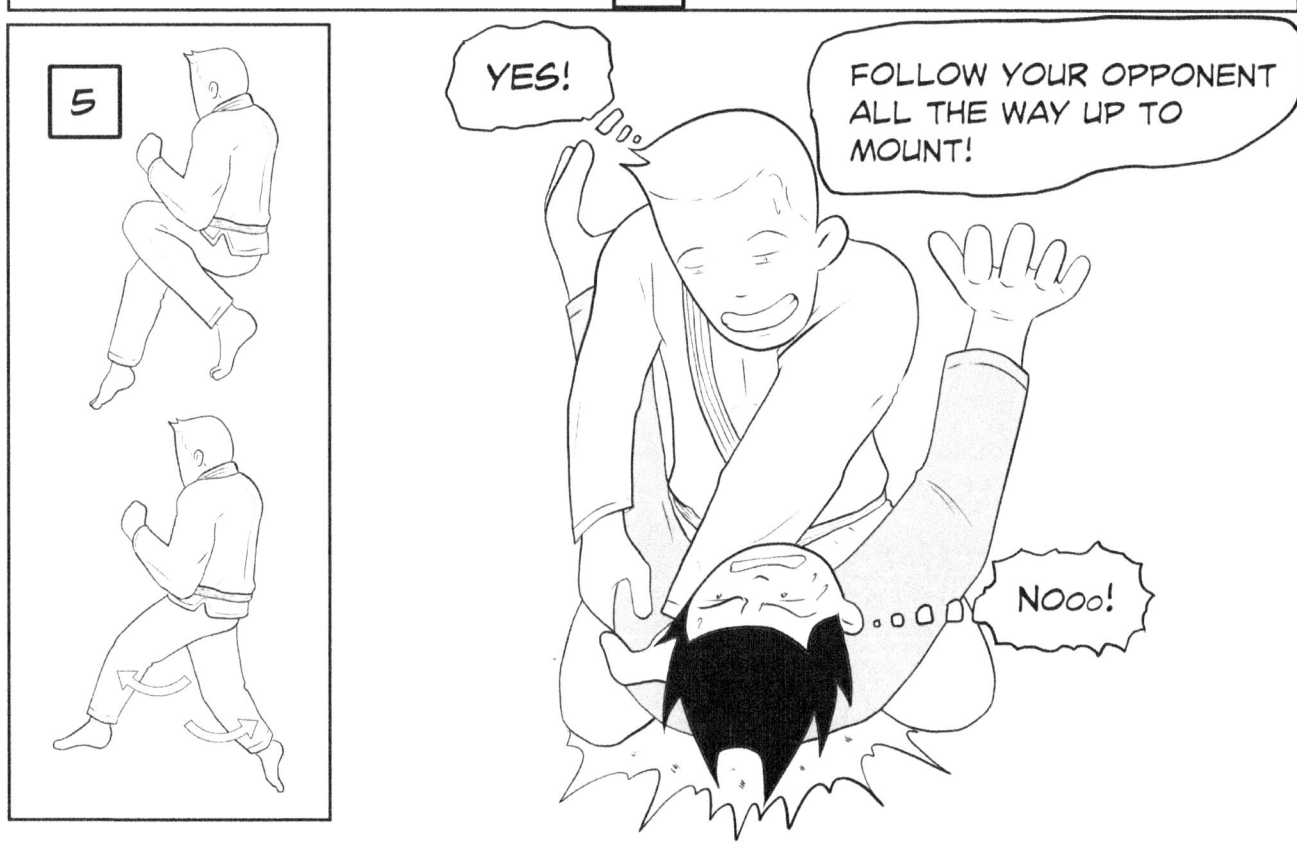

YES!

FOLLOW YOUR OPPONENT ALL THE WAY UP TO MOUNT!

NOoo!

HOW TO PRACTICE TECHNIQUES

1. When your instructor shows the class a new technique, pay close attention and make sure to ask questions.* Chances are, there are a few other students with the same questions.

2. When performing the technique, start out slow, cover all the steps of the technique. If you forget a step, make sure to ask the instructor for help. If you develop bad habit in practice, it will be very difficult to get rid of.

3. Once you have the steps down, try to smooth out the steps. For example, instead of doing the steps in 1,2,3,4, you will be doing the steps continuously in 1-4. You don't have to speed it up yet. You are just learning to do the move in a fluid manner.

4. Add a little bit of speed and explosiveness to your movement. If you are able to perform the technique well, add a little more.

5. Visualize how you would peform this technique against a resisting opponent. Think about how you might hold your grips, how much more you would exaggerate your movement. Now try to implement this into your practice.

If your technique starts to fall apart at any point, go back to the previous step and stay there until you're able to perform the technique well.

---

*Although most instructors welcome questions, there are some questions and statements that you should hold off on:

-What ifs: There is a what if situation that can be applied in any technique you learn in any martial art, because there are no move that you will learn that are 100% effective. If your instructor tried to teach you every little thing about a certain technique, class time will consist of your fellow students just listening and no one actually practicing. Trust your instructor that they are giving you the right amount of information needed for now. Try the technique in a roll. The problems you encounter in a roll are the what ifs you should be asking your instructor.

-I don't see how this will work: Being new to Jiu Jitsu, this question may come up from time to time. Keep an open mind. You just don't know enough about Jiu Jitsu to know what works and what doesn't. Again, put trust in your instructor that they know what they are doing. It's almost like blind faith but you have probably checked out your instructor and the academies ratings and reviews. If you try the technique with your training partner and are unable to perform the technique, ask your instructor for help at that time.

THINGS TO KEEP IN MIND DURING ROLLS
TAP EARLY, TAP OFTEN

If you get caught in a submission, make sure to tap early before your joint reaches full extension. There may not be much pain or discomfort until your joint locks out but the injury that follows is almost immediate.

If you wait for your joint to lock up to tap, you're tapping too late.

Tap at this point and you give your training partner time to release the submission safely.

TAP! TAP!

WAYS TO TAP:

Tap your training partner:
Make sure they can feel your tap.

Verbal tap:
Make sure your training partner can hear you loud and clear.

Tap the mat:
Make sure your training partner can hear the tap loud and clear.

You need to treat your training partners with respect and do everything you can to keep them safe during your rolls. Jiu Jitsu will be much more enjoyable if you have training partners that you share mutual respect with and both have regard for each other's safety.

Even if you are rolling at a fast pace, immediately slow down once you catch your submission. You need to exercise control and give your training partner plenty of time to tap.

THINGS TO KEEP IN MIND DURING ROLLS
IT'S OKAY NOT TO ROLL

Sometimes you shouldn't or can't roll and it's okay. It could be that you are recovering from an injury or you are too fatigued from training; what ever the reason, if you feel that it is not safe for you to roll, it's fine not to roll.

If you want to be active but avoid a full on roll, you could ask your training partner to drill a technique with you for the round, slow roll or positional spar.

Slow roll: Just like a regular roll but much slower. Don't rely on power or speed. Flow through your movements. Don't stay at one position for a prolonged period. If you catch a submission, release and continue the slow roll.

Positional spar: This is a great way to speed up your Jiu Jitsu progress. Pick a position that you feel safe to start in. Instead of rolling to a submission, pick an ending point such as guard pass or sweep.

THINGS TO KEEP IN MIND DURING ROLLS
ROLL WITH A PURPOSE

Rolling is fun. It's so much fun that sometimes you forget that there is a purpose to it other than just to have a great time joking around with your friends, trying to tap each other out. You can roll just for fun sometimes but most of the time, you should be rolling with a purpose.

Rolling with purpose:

80/20 rule: Roll 80% of the time with a game plan. You should have a list of techniques that you would like to work on during your rolls. Your goal during this time might not be to catch a submission. If it happens, its a added bonus but your goal for the roll could be as simple as maintaining open guard. In the beginning, your goal from bottom guard during your rolls will most likely be to not let your training partners pass your guard. From top, not to get swept or submitted.

20% of the time, go after your training partners and have fun!

Fake it till you make it:

In the beginning, most moves, possibly all the techniques you try against your training partners in a roll, will fail. This can lead you into a negative mindset where you expect failure from any technique you attempt. A mediocre technique that you attempt with 100% belief will have significantly better success rate than a good technique that you attempt with uncertainty. Even if you know that your technique is not yet great, even if you failed countless times, believe in your technique every time you go for your move.

Roll consistently:

Make a commitment to yourself and keep yourself accountable. You can sit around whenever you want. When you are at your academy, get your rolls in. If you don't have the cardio to roll continuously through the rounds, try taking every other round off.

THINGS TO KEEP IN MIND DURING ROLLS
ROLL WITH A PURPOSE

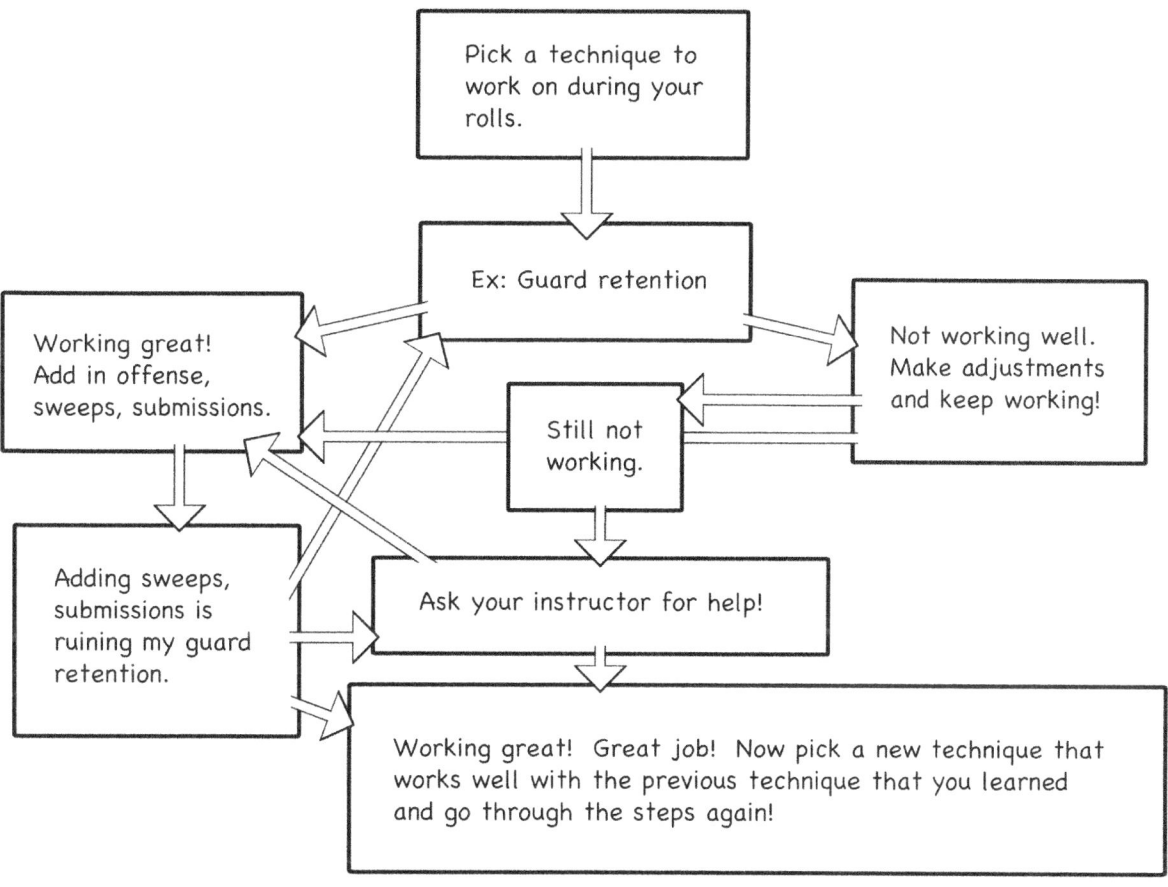

Stay focused. Jiu Jitsu has an overwhelming amount of techniques. You will be exposed to new techniques all the time at your academy, on social media and in books. Choose a few techniques that you want to invest your time into, stick with it for a while until you feel it is time to move on. The exception is in class, when your instructor is teaching you a technique that has nothing to do with what it is that you are working on, still participate with full attention.

ROLL GOALS!

STARTING FROM TOP → **STARTING FROM BOTTOM**

↓

ESTABLISH GRIPS.

↓ (top branch) / ↓ (bottom branch)

Top branch:

- MAINTAIN TOP POSITION. AVOID SUBMISSIONS AND SWEEPS.
- SETUP YOUR GUARD PASS.
- PASS YOUR OPPONENT'S GUARD.

Bottom branch:

- ESTABLISH GUARD.
- BREAK DOWN YOUR OPPONENT'S POSTURE AND SETUP YOUR OFFENSE USING SUBMISSIONS, SWEEPS AND BACK TAKE.
- IF YOU SWEPT YOUR OPPONENT, IT'S TIME TO ATTACK FROM TOP!

↓ (both branches merge)

- SETTLE INTO YOUR ADVANTAGE POSITION. AS A BEGINNER I RECOMMEND HOLDING EACH POSITION AFTER THE GUARD PASS MINIMUM OF 30 SECONDS TO LEARN HOW TO LOCKDOWN YOUR OPPONENT.

↓

- IMPROVE POSITION OR START SETTING UP YOUR SUBMISSIONS

↓

- CATCH SUBMISSIONS.

↓

- APPLY SUBMISSIONS SLOWLY. NOT ONLY IS THIS FOR THE SAFETY OF YOUR TRAINING PARTNERS, THIS WILL HELP YOU BUILD CONTROL OVER YOUR SUBMISSIONS.

THANK YOU FOR READING!

I was first introduced to Jiu Jitsu by my friends in a form of watching old school no holds barred fighting. I was instantly captivated by it. After a few sessions of wrestling my friends in their living room, I knew that I wanted to learn Jiu Jitsu. As I trained Jiu Jitsu and watched more fights, I had a dream of fighting in the cage like my Jiu Jitsu heroes and someday earning my black belt. As a 23 year old in 2001, it seemed like impossible dreams. I'm so grateful that I have gotten to reach these goals and that I now get to teach Jiu Jitsu for a living.

I hope Jiu Jitsu becomes as special a part of your life as it has for me!

Keisuke Andrew

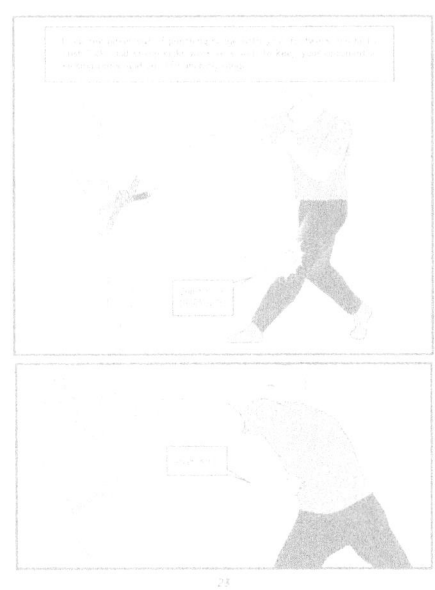

LEG TRIP TAKEDOWN

HIGH DOUBLE LEG TAKEDOWN

JIU JITSU FIGHT STRATEGIES

 **KEISUKE ANDREW**

48 PAGES

Copyright © 2020 by Keisuke Andrew
All rights reserved. This book or any portion thereof
may not be reproduced or used in any manner whatsoever
without the express written permission of the author
except for the use of brief quotations in a book review.

The information in this book is meant to supplement, not replace, proper martial arts training. Like any sport, martial arts involving speed, equipment, balance and environmental factors poses some inherent risk. The author advises readers to take full responsibility for their safety and know their limits. Before practicing the skills described in this book, be sure that you do not take risks beyond your level of experience, aptitude, training and comfort level. Only practice under the strict supervision of a qualified instructor.

Foreword

One of my favorite things about Jiu Jitsu is dissecting my opponent's strengths and weaknesses and coming up with a strategy to defeat my opponent. With the right strategy a person might be able to defeat an opponent that under normal circumstances they would have no chance of beating. With this book, I wanted to touch on some of the basic strategies on fighting using Jiu Jitsu.

I would like to clarify that this book is not a depiction or glorification of street fighting. I believe that physical altercation should be the last resort when you have to protect yourself or others. I am a fight fan when it is two combatants, who have honed their skills and have agreed to mutual combat in a regulated format, whether it is sparring at an MMA school or a formal match in a ring or cage

Thank you for taking the time to pick up this book. I hope it will help guide you in your Jiu Jitsu journey. If you could rate and/or review this book I would greatly appreciate it! If you are ever in Oregon City, Oregon, I would love for you to come visit Enso Jiu Jitsu!

Keisuke Andrew

About the Author

Keisuke started training Brazilian Jiu Jitsu and Mixed martial arts in 2001 and received his Black belt in 2009. In MMA competition, Keisuke has amassed a record of 5-0 in amateur competition and 3-0 as a pro. Keisuke is the head Instructor of Enso Jiu Jitsu, his own Brazilian Jiu Jitsu Academy in Oregon City, Oregon.

TABLE OF CONTENTS

CHAPTER 1: NOVICE STREET FIGHTER VS JIU JITSU   4

CHAPTER 2: JIU JITSU VS BOXING   20

CHAPTER 3: GIANT VS JIU JITSU   34

NOVICE STREET FIGHTER VS JIU JITSU

Do not underestimate your opponent because anyone can get lucky with a punchers chance!

First, collect information about your opponent. Step in and out within your safety distance to see how they react. Do they react, over react; do they step back or come forward? How well do they move? Next, throw a light jab towards their face from a safe distance, not to actually hit your opponent but to see how they react. Pay attention to see if they flinch, freeze, back up, come forward or try to hit you.

Side step left and right to see how your opponent does with angle changes. Make sure to keep appropriate distance, especially moving towards their rear hand as that is the side that they can throw punches and kicks with maximum power.

What is he doing?

Level change to see how they react to takedown threat!

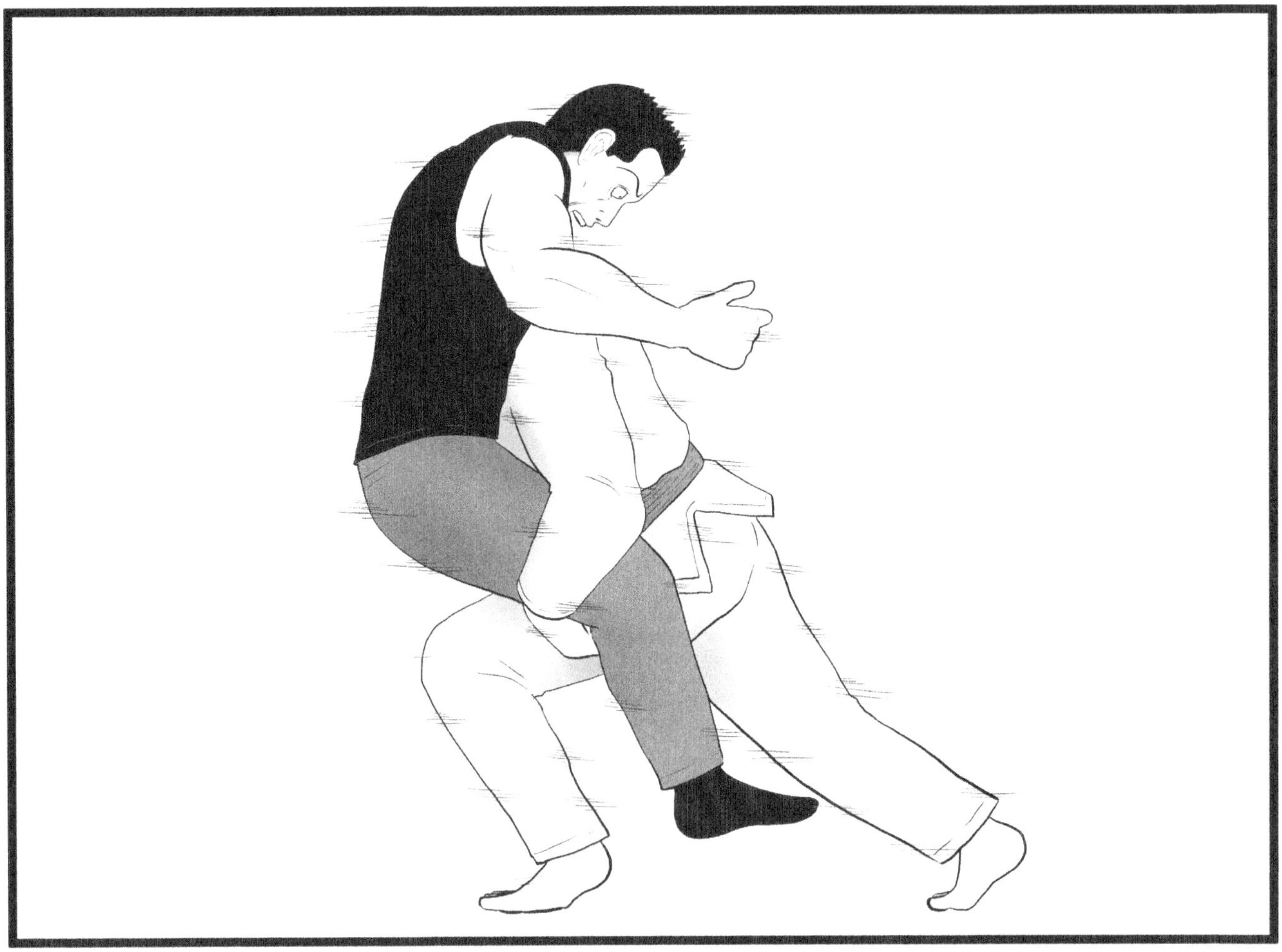

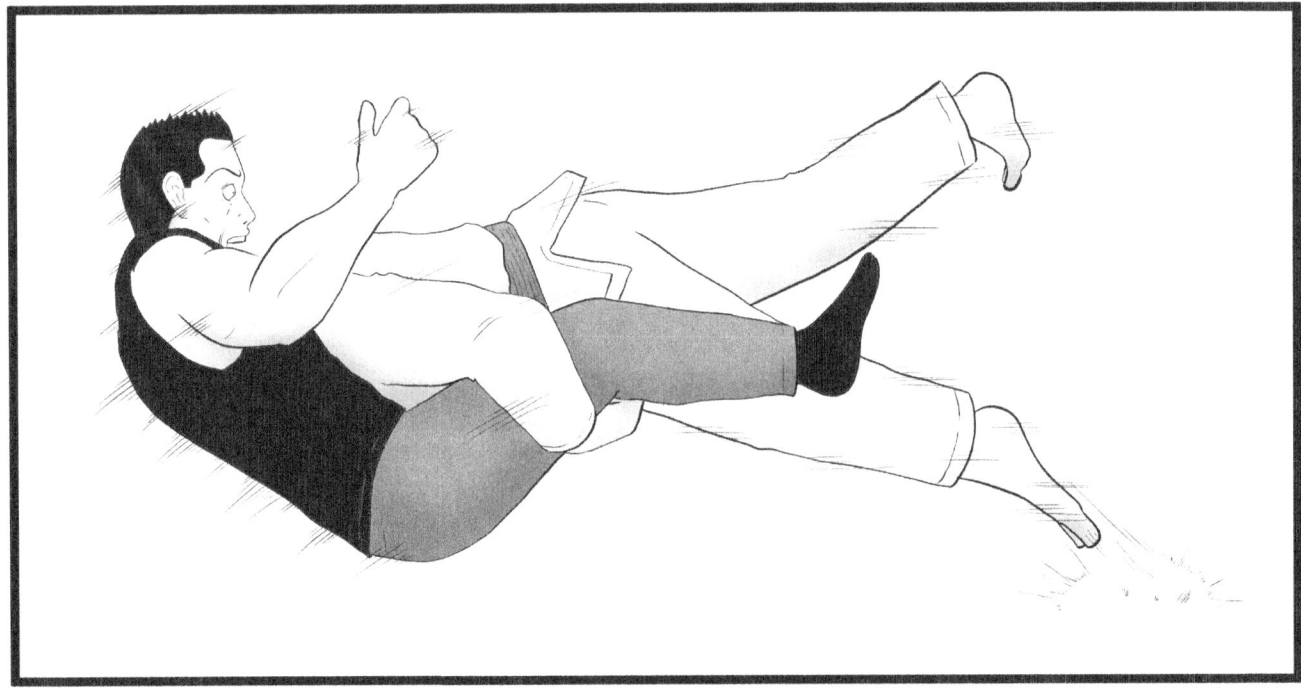

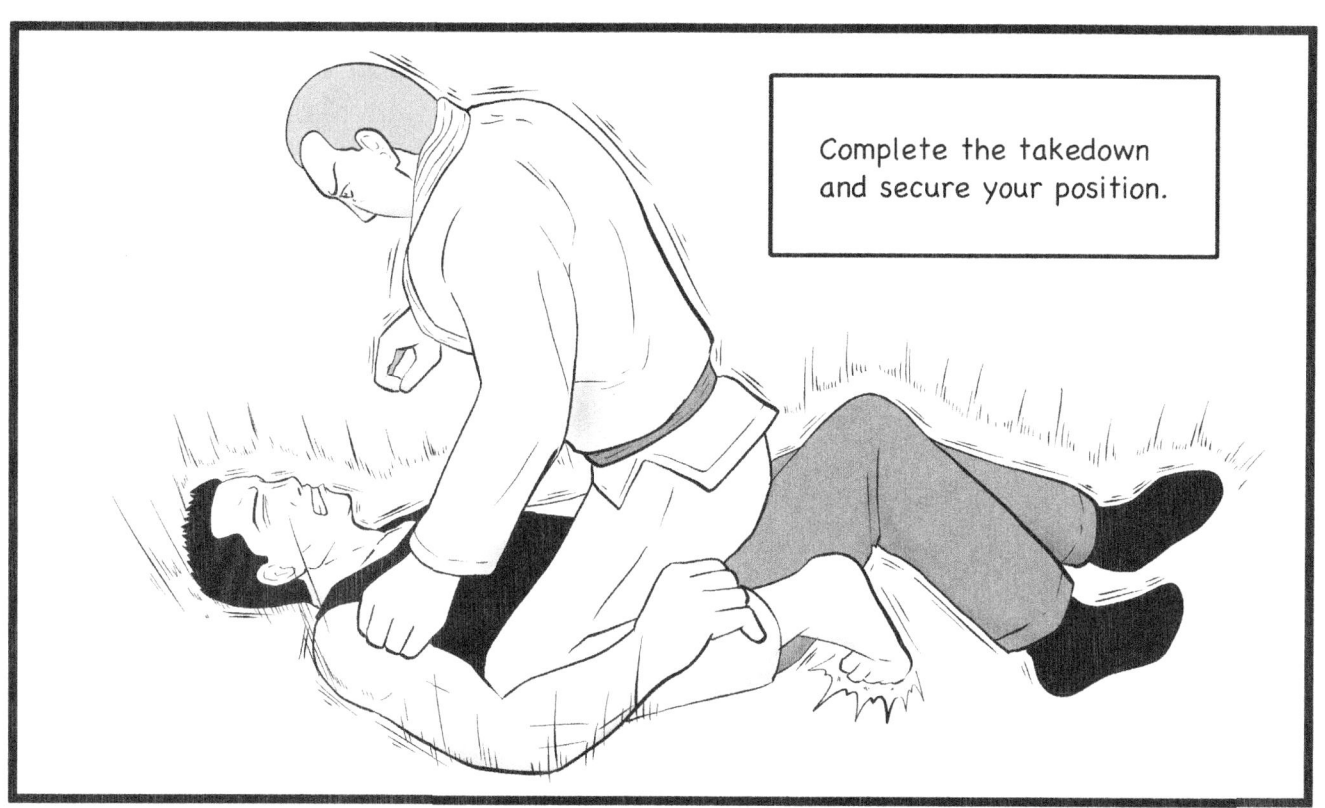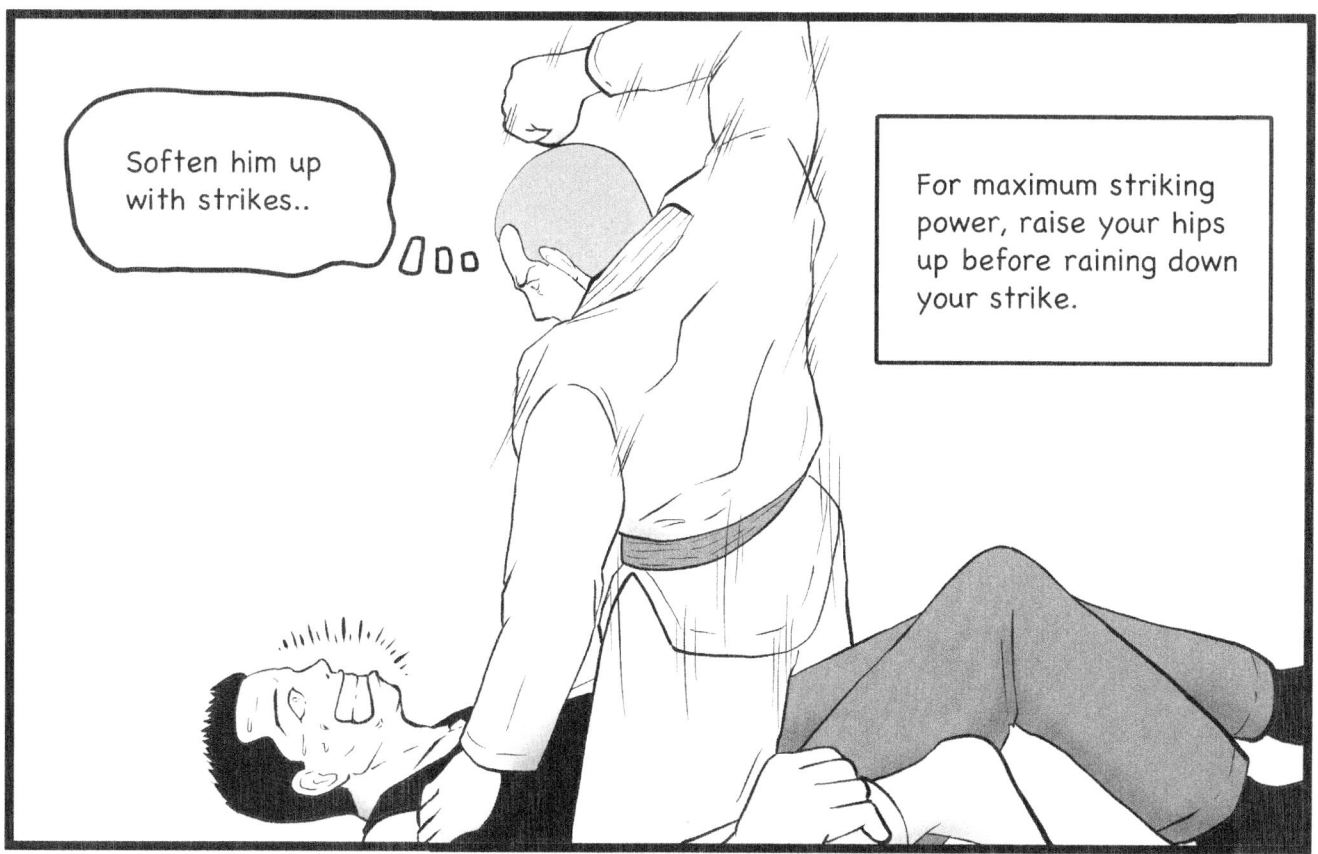

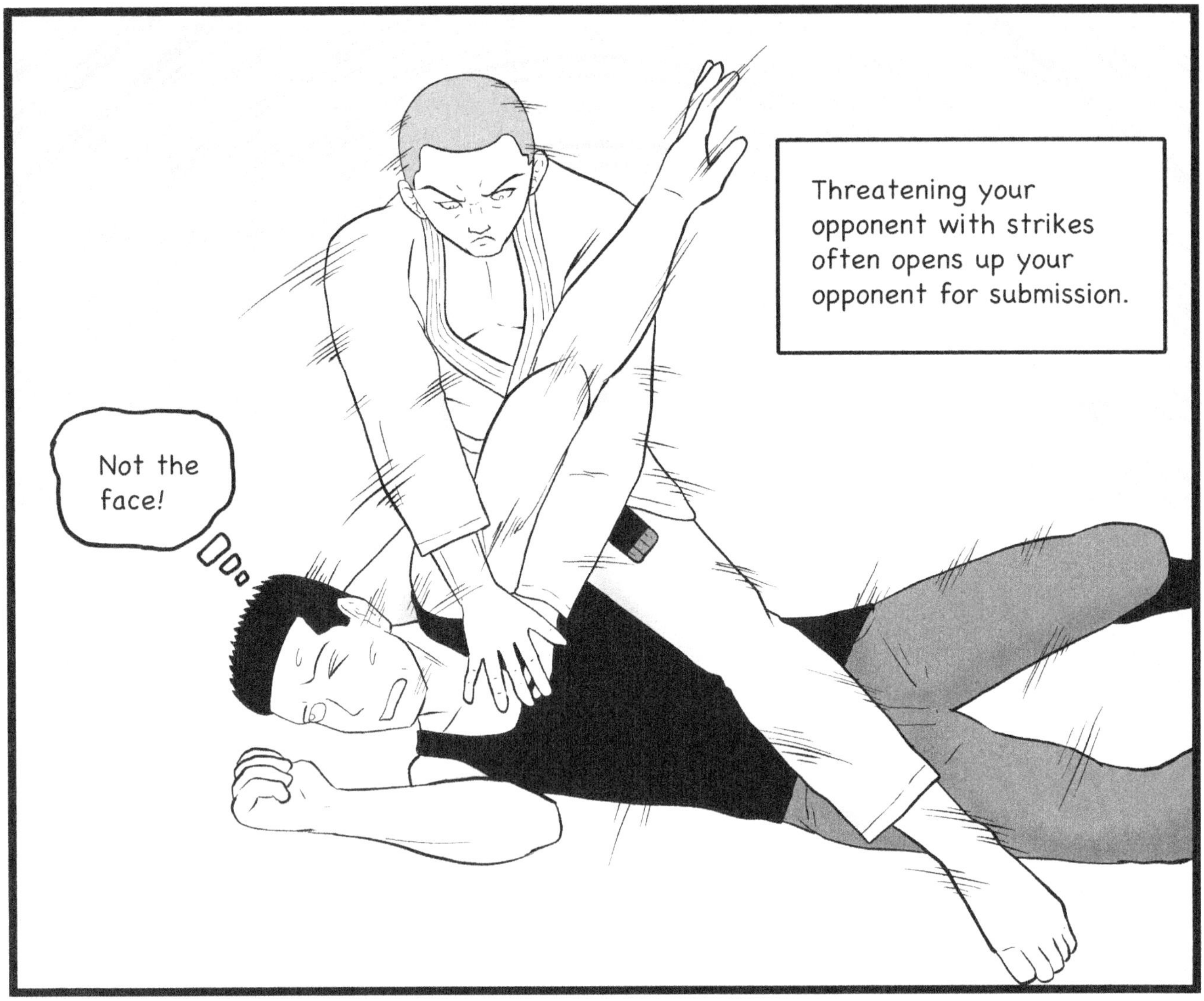

FIGHT TECHNIQUE BREAKDOWN!

In this chapter, you will see instructions for positions where the characters are described doing movements on just one side. The positions can be done on either side but has been illustrated on just one side for simplicity.

FROM THE BOOK BEGINNER'S JIU JITSU GUIDE!

In a fight, you have to minimize your opponent's chance of hurting you and give yourself the best chance of ending the fight. The biggest hurdle is closing the gap between you and your opponent where they have the best chance of landing a strike and taking them down.

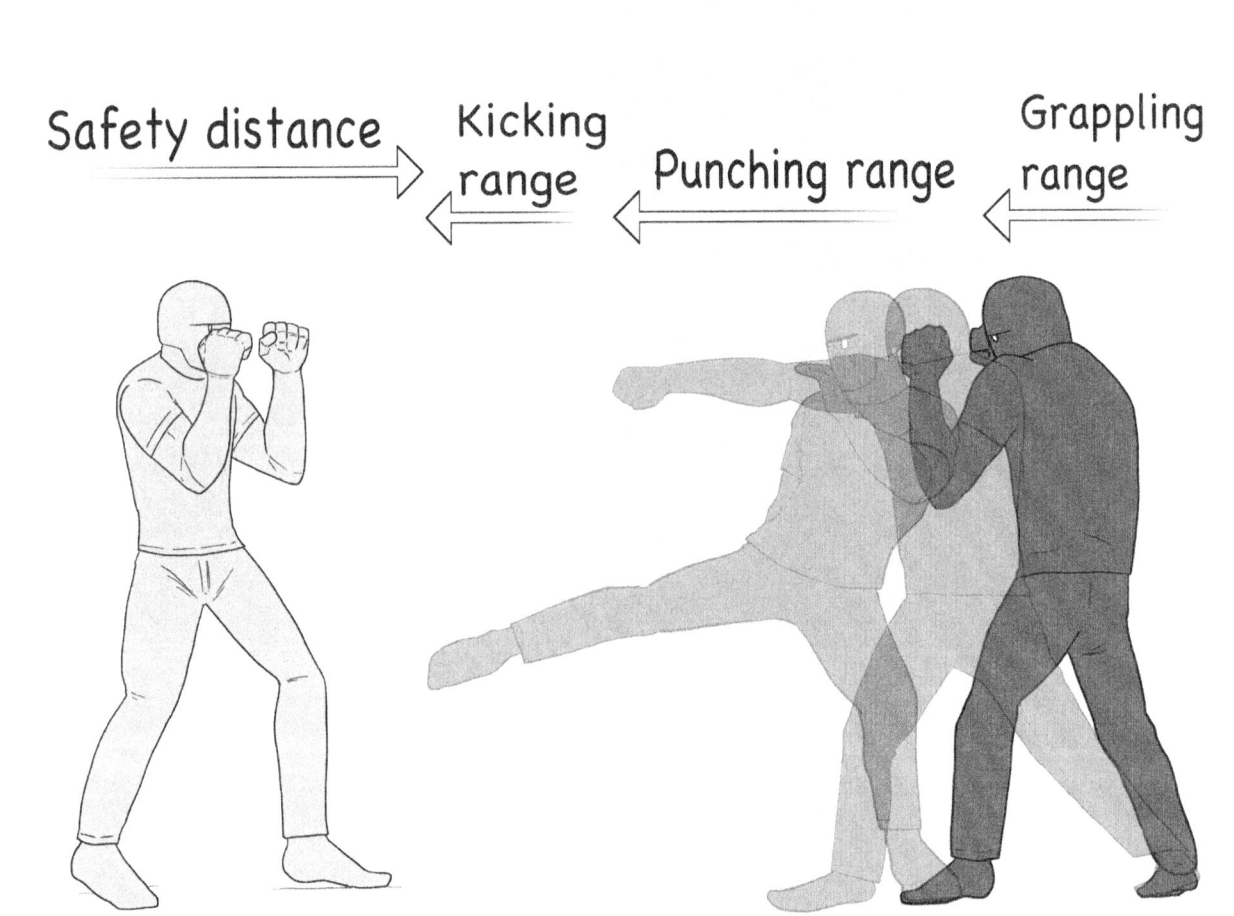

Between the punching range and grappling range is also the range where you can get kneed, elbowed or taken down yourself. Until you are 100% ready to commit to closing in on your opponent, you have to maintain your safety distance with your footwork and strikes of your own.

FROM THE BOOK BEGINNER'S JIU JITSU GUIDE!

Throwing punches without gloves can be devastating to your hand but, just by threatening your opponent by putting your jabs out will help keep your opponent away and will make it significantly easier to get into your grappling range.

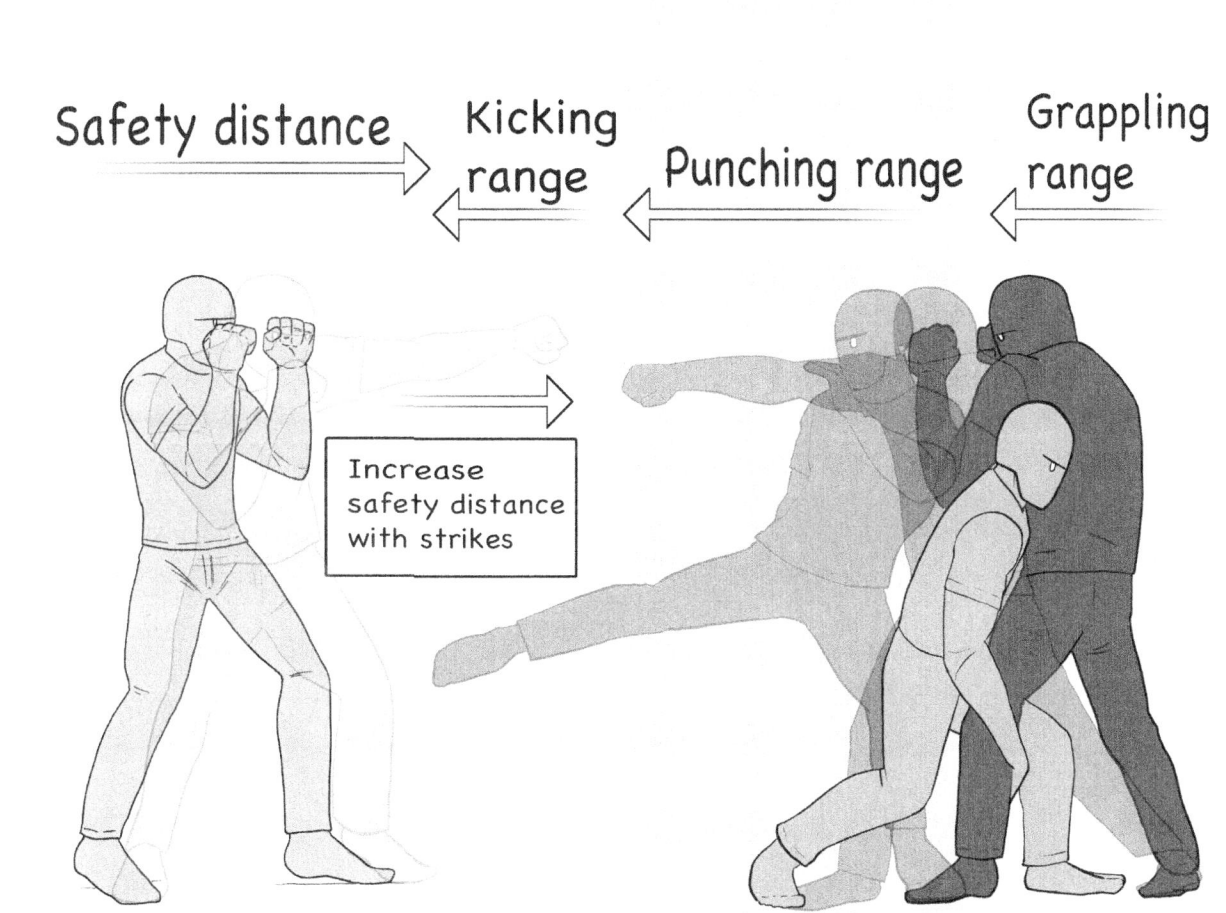

Pay close attention to how your opponent throws strikes, how they move and how they react when you fake a jab or fake a takedown. This will give you valuable information about your opponent's tendencies and when it is safe to close the gap.

HIGH DOUBLE LEG TAKEDOWN

1. Setting up your takedown entry with strikes will increase your success rate significantly. Throw your lead hand into your opponent's face. Step in deep to close the gap between you and your opponent.

2. Drive your left shoulder into your opponent's torso. Keep your head up as even a novice fighter will snatch your neck if it is easily accessible.

3. Grab both legs behind the calves. Keep your elbows in tight to prevent your opponent from getting underhooks.

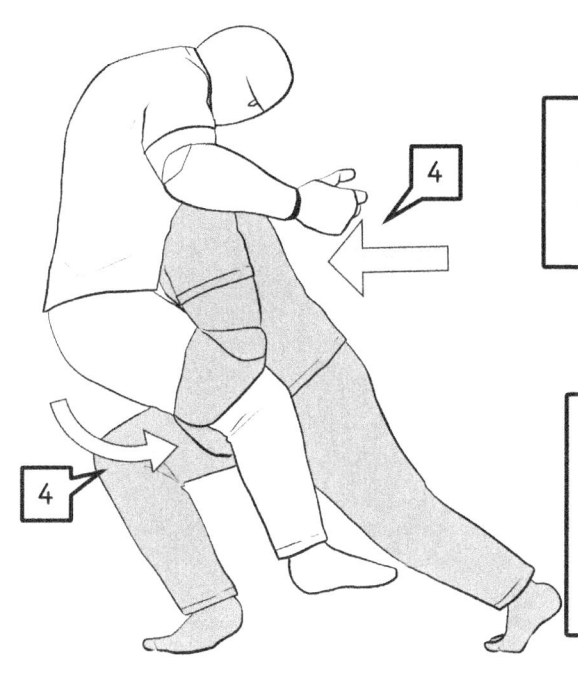

4. Push with your shoulder and pull the legs as you drive forward.

5. Follow your opponent down to the ground. Stay connected to your opponent with your left shoulder. Be careful not to land on your face. Use your opponent as a landing pad.

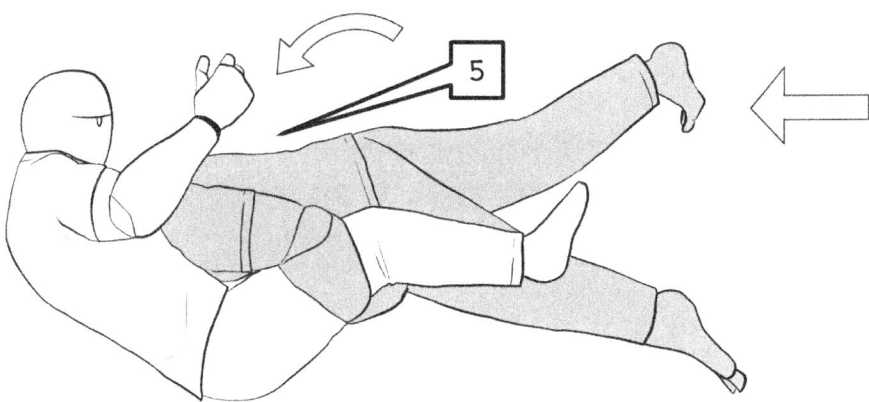

6. Secure your position by driving your toes into the ground and transferring the pressure into your left shoulder, pinning your opponent to the ground.

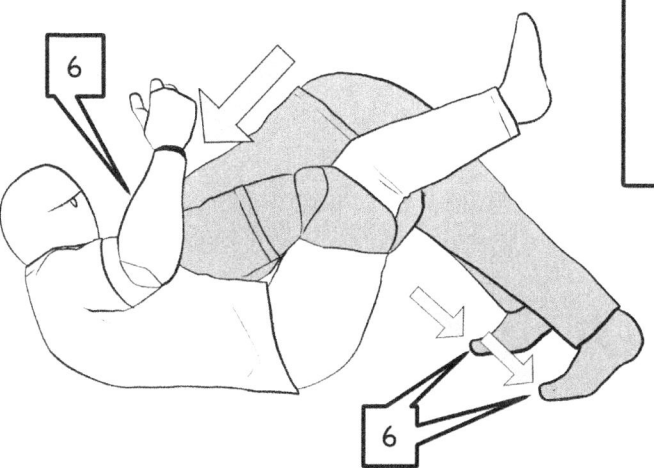

FROM THE BOOK !

ARMBAR

1. When your opponent pushes, left hand comes around your opponent's right arm. Your right hand comes between your opponent's arms towards the center of the chest.

2. Put your hands together and shift your weight into your hands. As the weight shifts from your legs and hips into your hands, your hips and legs should move freely. Spin to the left.

3. Your left knee will be right by your opponent's head. Your right leg will be staying behind by your opponent's left hip.

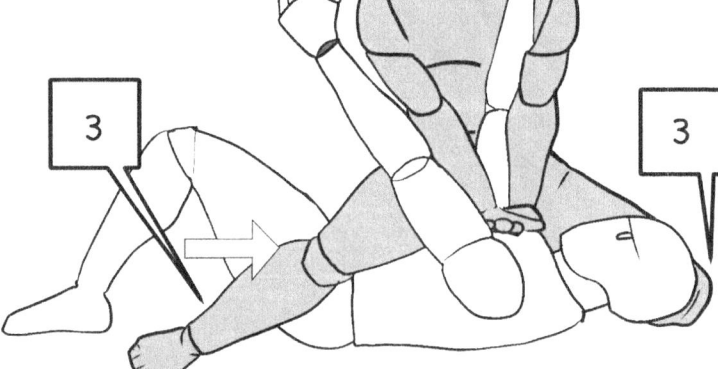

FROM THE BOOK !

5. Keep pressing your weight into your hands. Move your right leg into the armpit of your opponent.

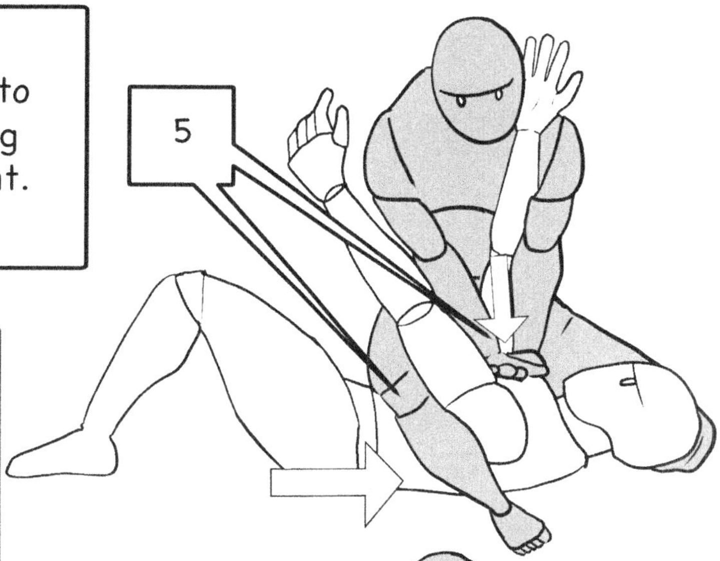

6. Transfer your weight from your hands to your right thigh by shifting your right shoulder towards your opponent's left hip. This should lighten up the weight of your left leg. Move your left leg over your opponent's head.

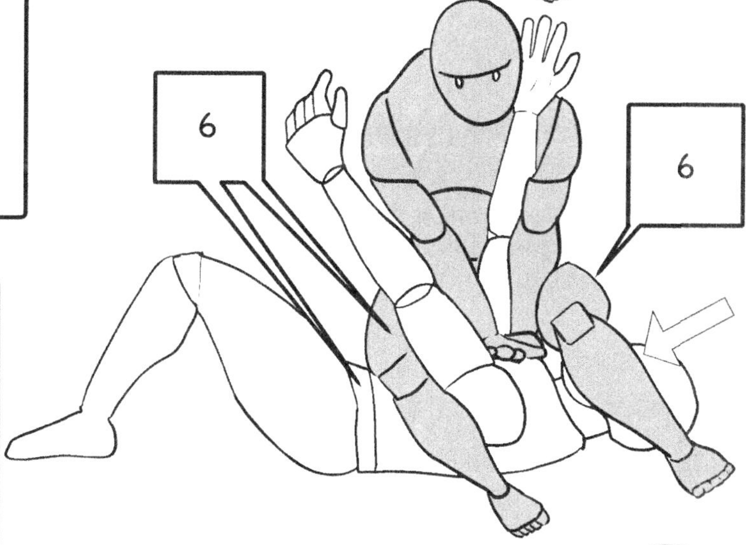

7. Hug your opponent's arm near you, sit on the ground slowly with control. Pinch your knees tight together to lock up your opponent's arm. Bring your heels towards you to lock up your opponent's head and torso. Pull your opponent's arm back slowly till it locks out.

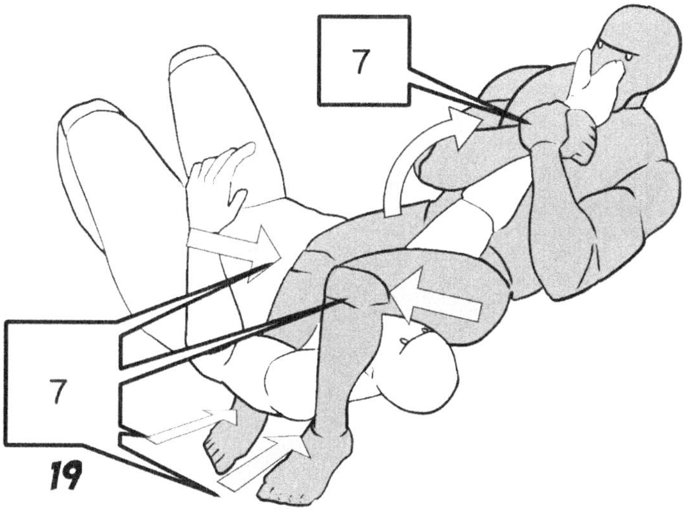

JIU JITSU VS BOXING

Patient and cautious boxers who try to pick you apart from a distance can be very difficult to defeat. Aggressive and over confident boxers are much easier to takedown.

CRACK!

Punching range belongs to the boxers. If you stay there a moment too long, they will make you pay.

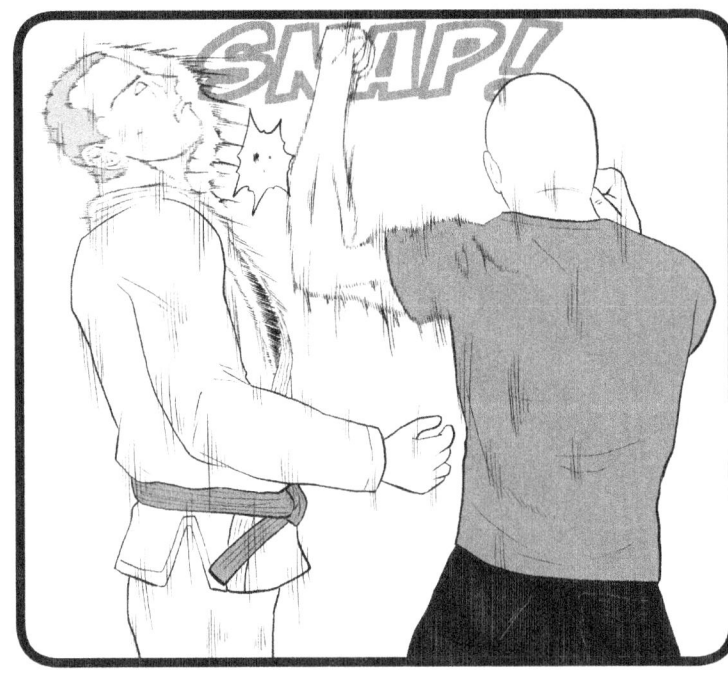

SNAP!

Keep the boxer out of punching range with your footwork and kicks. Push kicks and stomp kicks work very well to keep your opponent in kicking range and out of punching range.

Joint Kick
(関節蹴り)

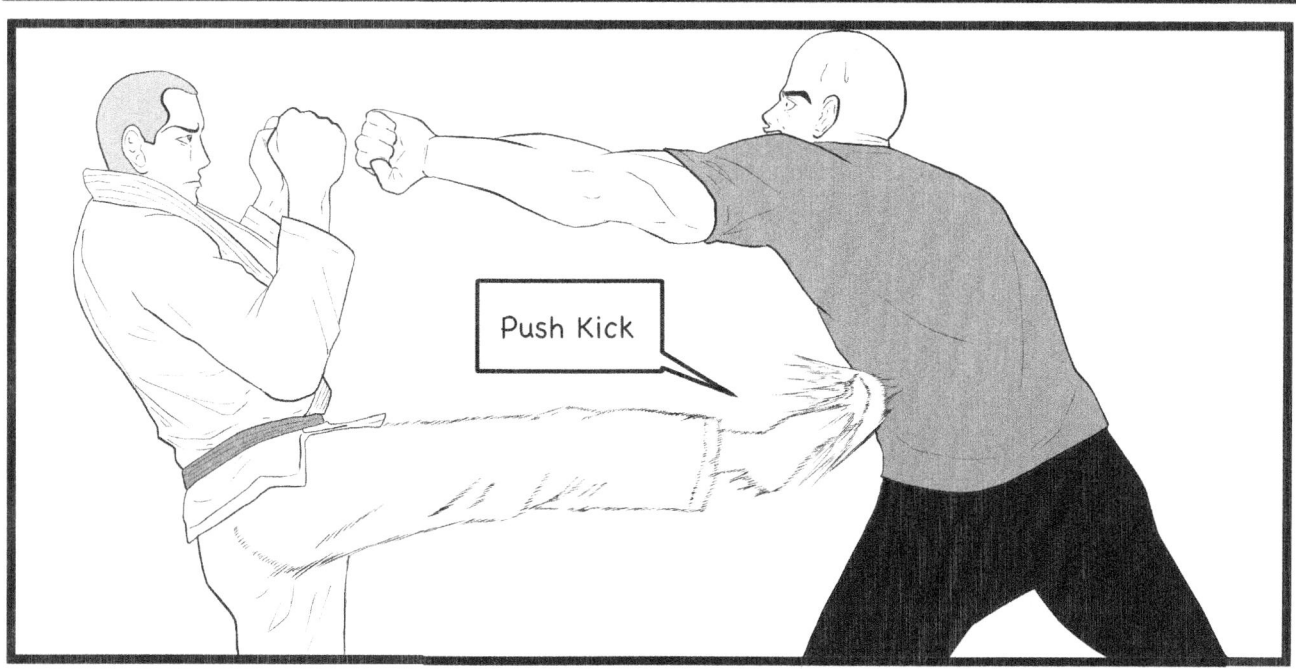

Push Kick

If you can make the boxer chase you, it will make it easier to get through their punching range, right to the grappling range.

When your opponent overcommits to the chase, shoot in for the takedown.

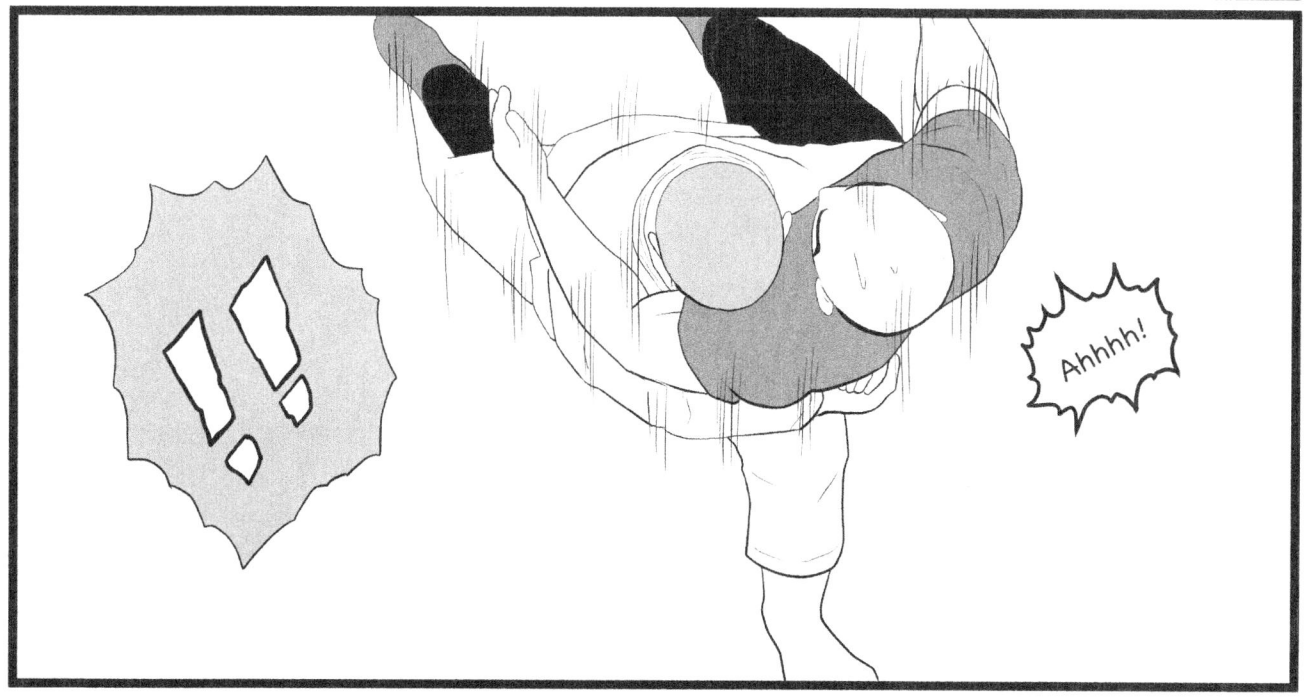

25

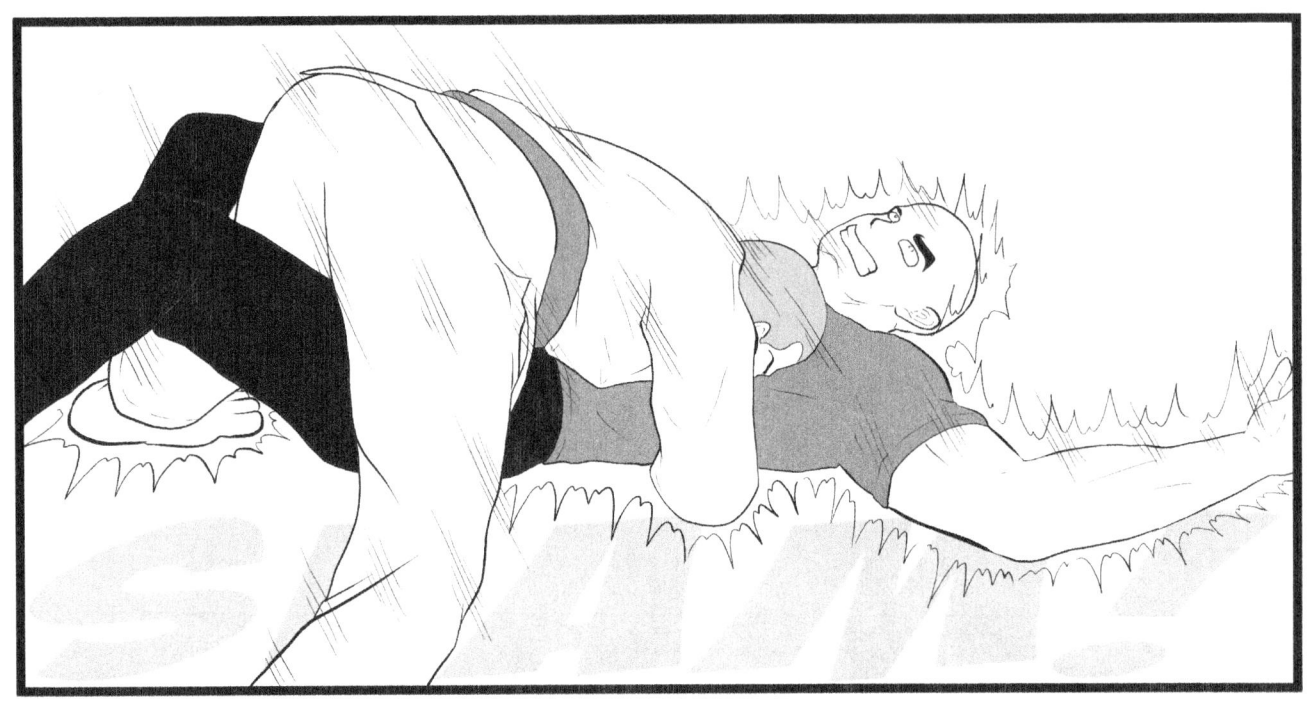

When you're in a dominant position like mount, many options open up. In the previous fight against the novice fighter, the purple belt went for a armbar in this position. Against the boxer here, he is setting up a back take. Your next move depends on how your opponent tries to escape this position or on how you setup your opponent.

If your opponent exposes their limbs for a chance at a high percentage finish rate submission, the choice is obvious. When there is a chance for a submission but you are unsure if you can pull it off, the safe choice is to improve position and then look for a higher percentage submission.

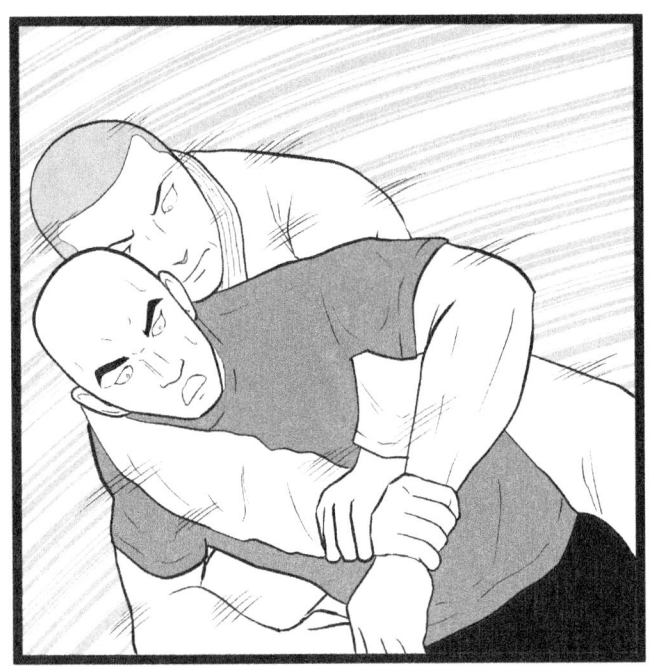

...tap...

FIGHT TECHNIQUE BREAKDOWN!

In this chapter, you will see instructions for positions where the characters are described doing movements on just one side. The positions can be done on either side but has been illustrated on just one side for simplicity.

LEG TRIP TAKEDOWN

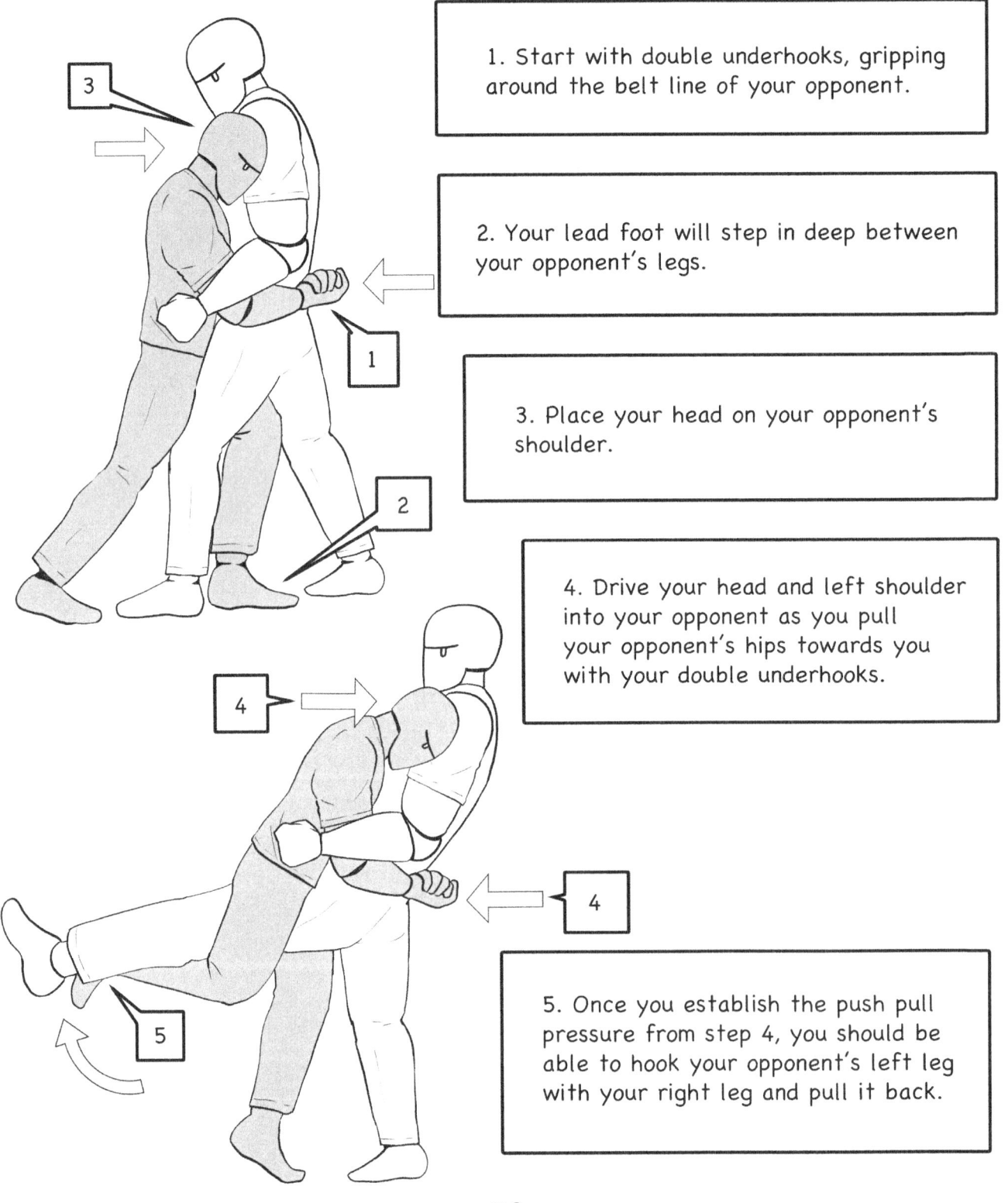

1. Start with double underhooks, gripping around the belt line of your opponent.

2. Your lead foot will step in deep between your opponent's legs.

3. Place your head on your opponent's shoulder.

4. Drive your head and left shoulder into your opponent as you pull your opponent's hips towards you with your double underhooks.

5. Once you establish the push pull pressure from step 4, you should be able to hook your opponent's left leg with your right leg and pull it back.

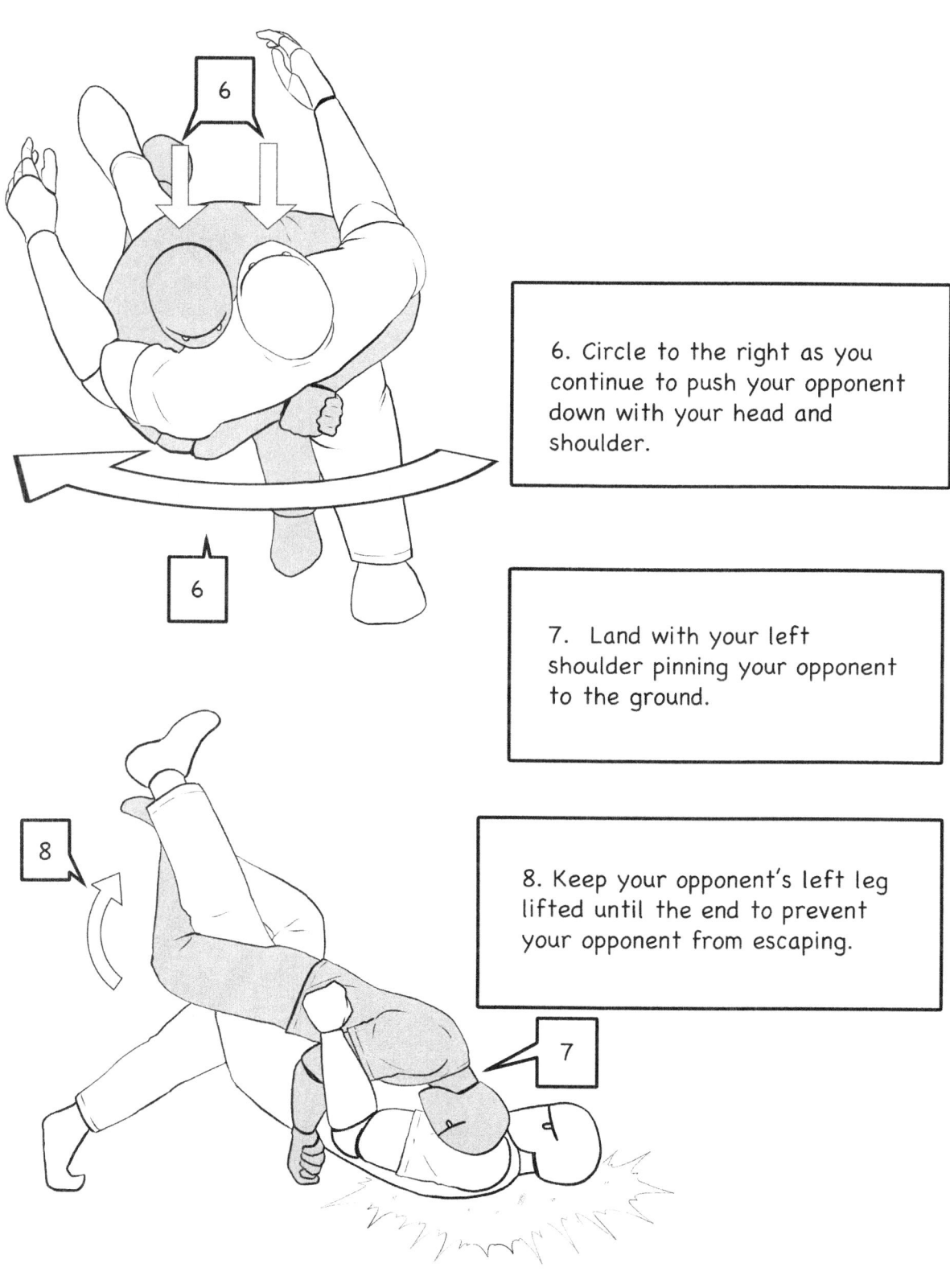

6. Circle to the right as you continue to push your opponent down with your head and shoulder.

7. Land with your left shoulder pinning your opponent to the ground.

8. Keep your opponent's left leg lifted until the end to prevent your opponent from escaping.

FROM THE BOOK BEGINNER'S JIU JITSU GUIDE!
REAR NAKED CHOKE

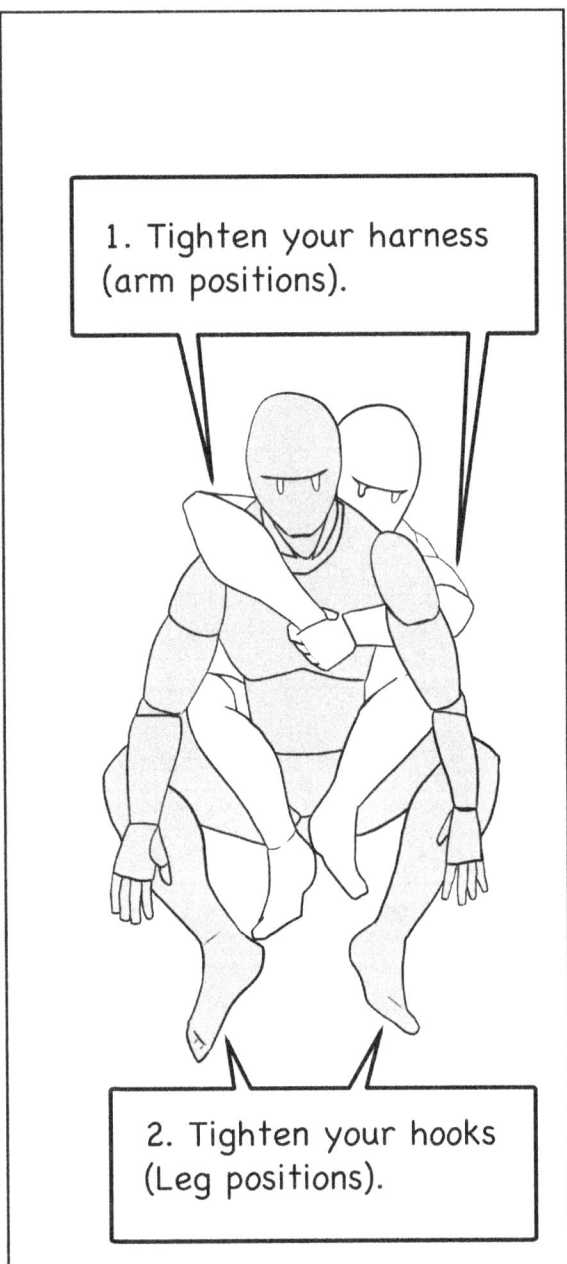

1. Tighten your harness (arm positions).

2. Tighten your hooks (Leg positions).

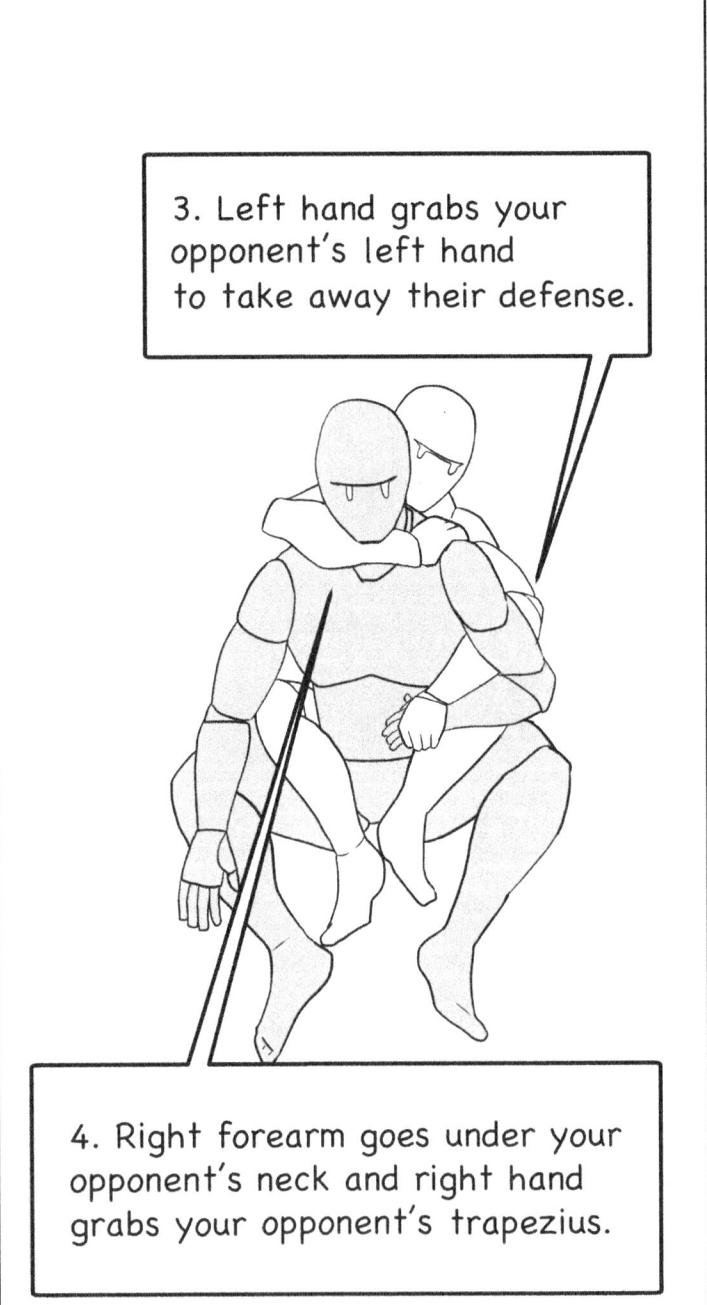

3. Left hand grabs your opponent's left hand to take away their defense.

4. Right forearm goes under your opponent's neck and right hand grabs your opponent's trapezius.

FROM THE BOOK !

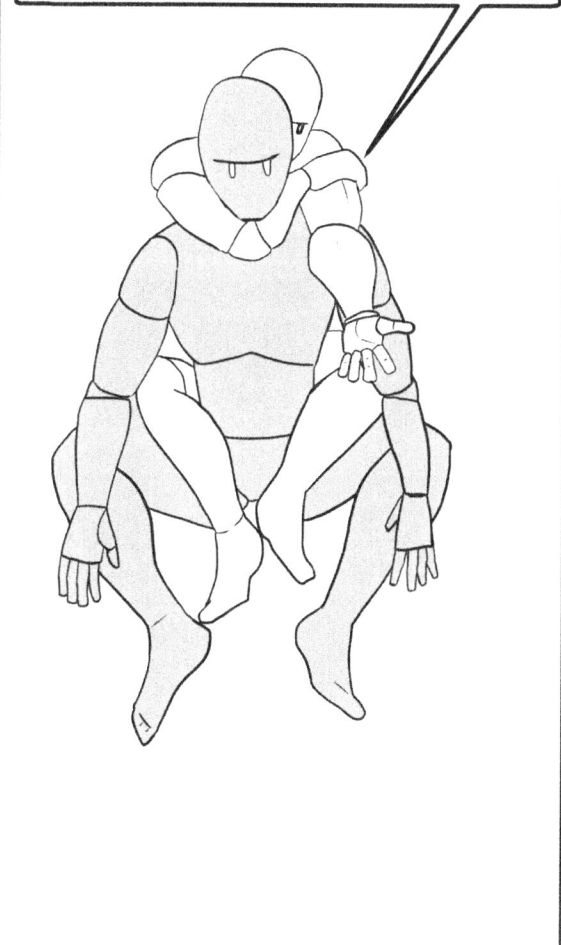

5. Right hand grabs your left bicep as deep as possible. Right elbow should be aligned with your opponent's chin.

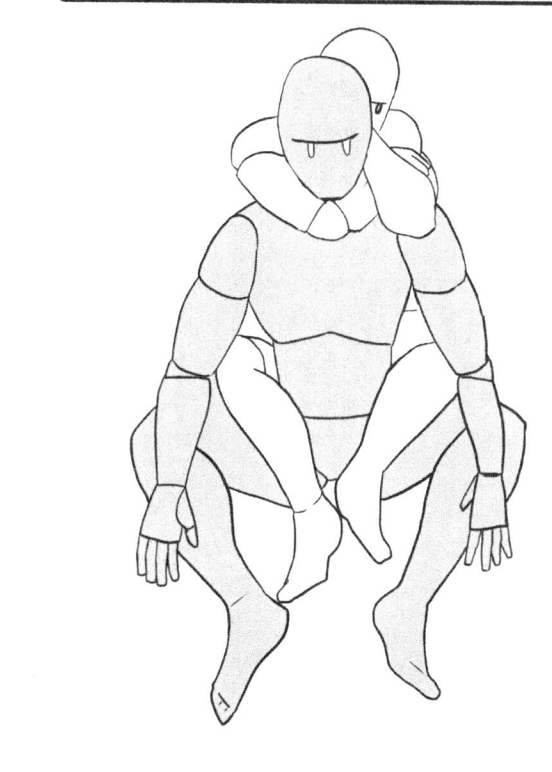

6. Left hand comes behind your opponents head, palm down, reaching towards your right shoulder. Squeeze slowly with your arms. With your left arm, push your opponent's head towards your right elbow to complete the choke.

GIANT
VS
JIU JITSU

When fighting a giant, patience becomes the key to surviving and possibly defeating the giant. If you try to push the pace at the wrong time and get exhausted, they will crush you with ease.

Even a light strike from a heavyweight can put you down. The fight could be over when you get knocked down if you do not know how to breakfall. Make sure its second nature for you to fall safely when you get knocked down!

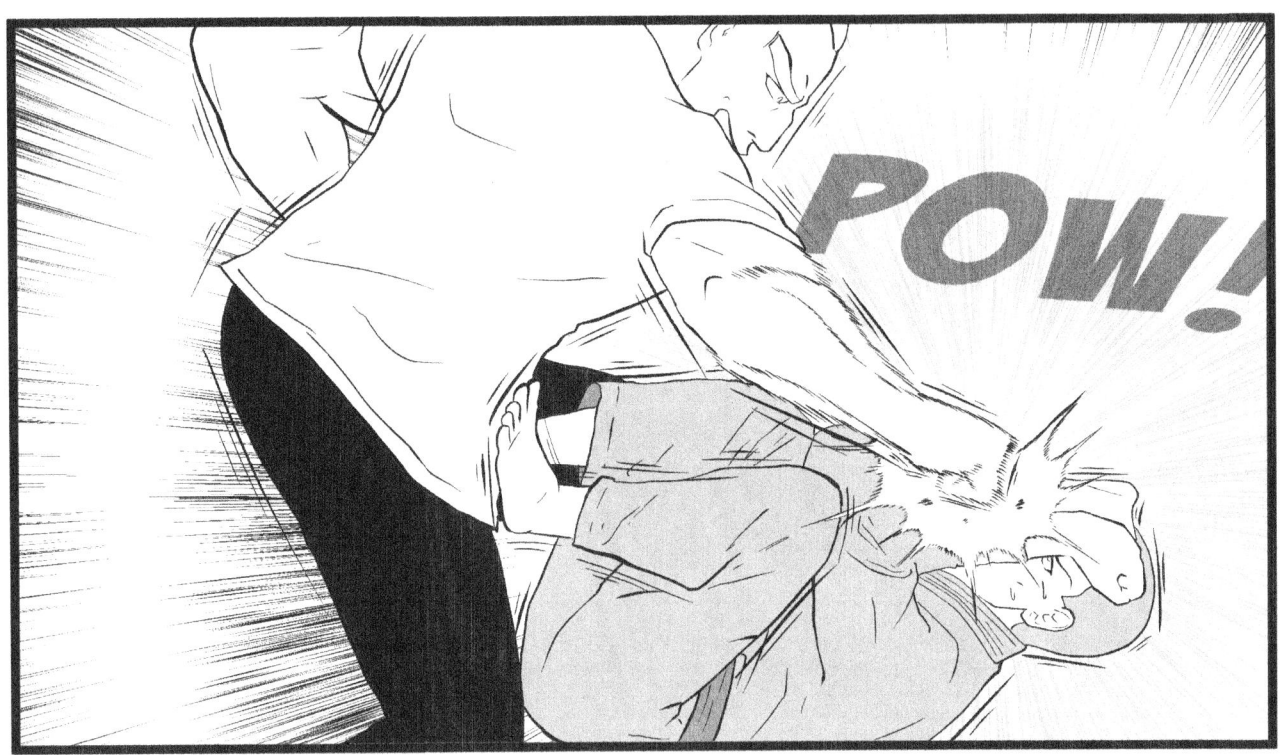

Use your legs to push your opponent away to create your safety space. Your opponent will have difficulty connecting with strikes if you keep your legs extended.

If your opponent forces through your legs to throw a strike, be ready to trap your opponent's arm with an overhook. Tie up your opponent with overhooks to prevent them from effectively striking.

To setup an overhook off of your opponent's strike, drive your hand up right next to your opponent's head with your palm facing out. This will slide your opponent's punch down your arm. Make sure to protect your jaw by keeping your shoulder high. Once your opponent's arm has slid down, trap the arm in an overhook.

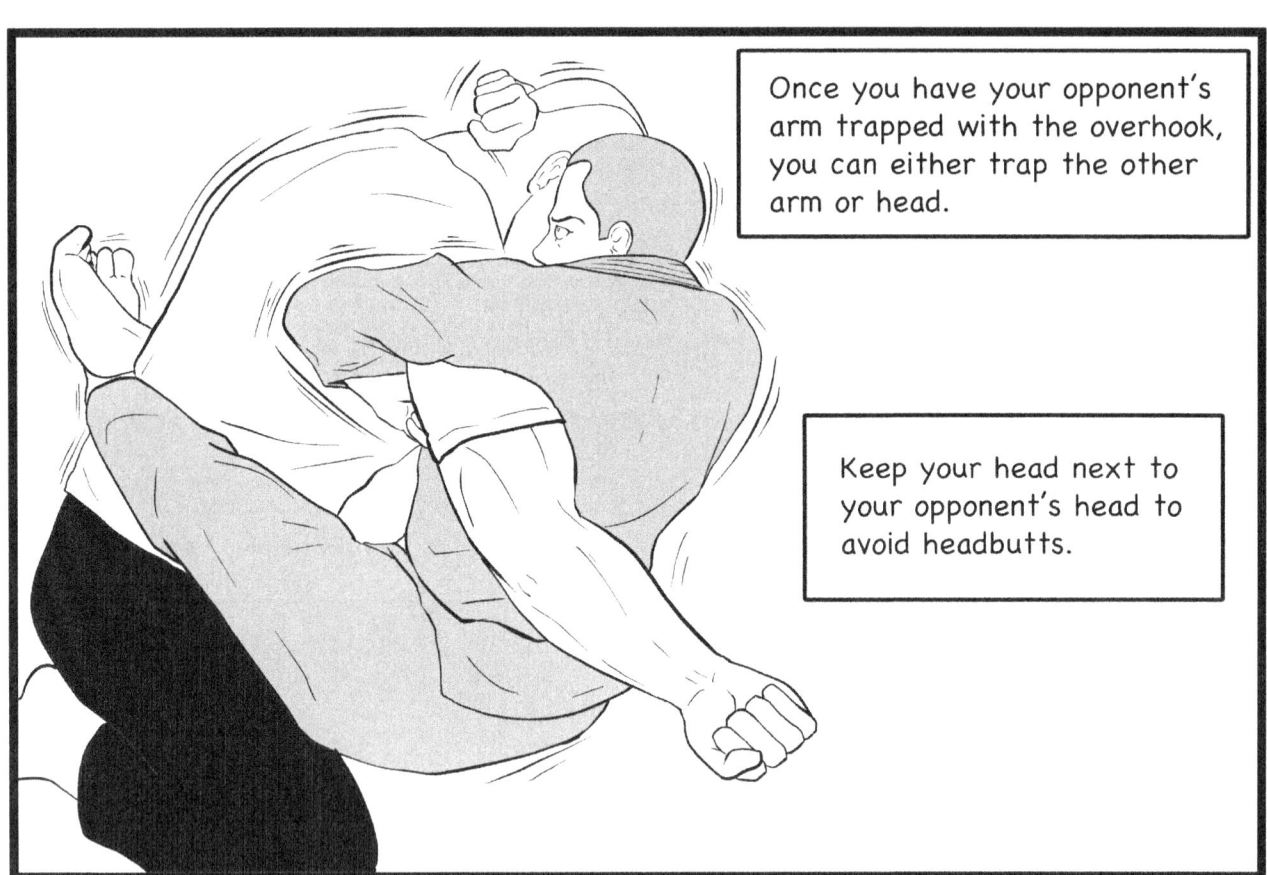

Once you have your opponent's arm trapped with the overhook, you can either trap the other arm or head.

Keep your head next to your opponent's head to avoid headbutts.

Let go of my arm!

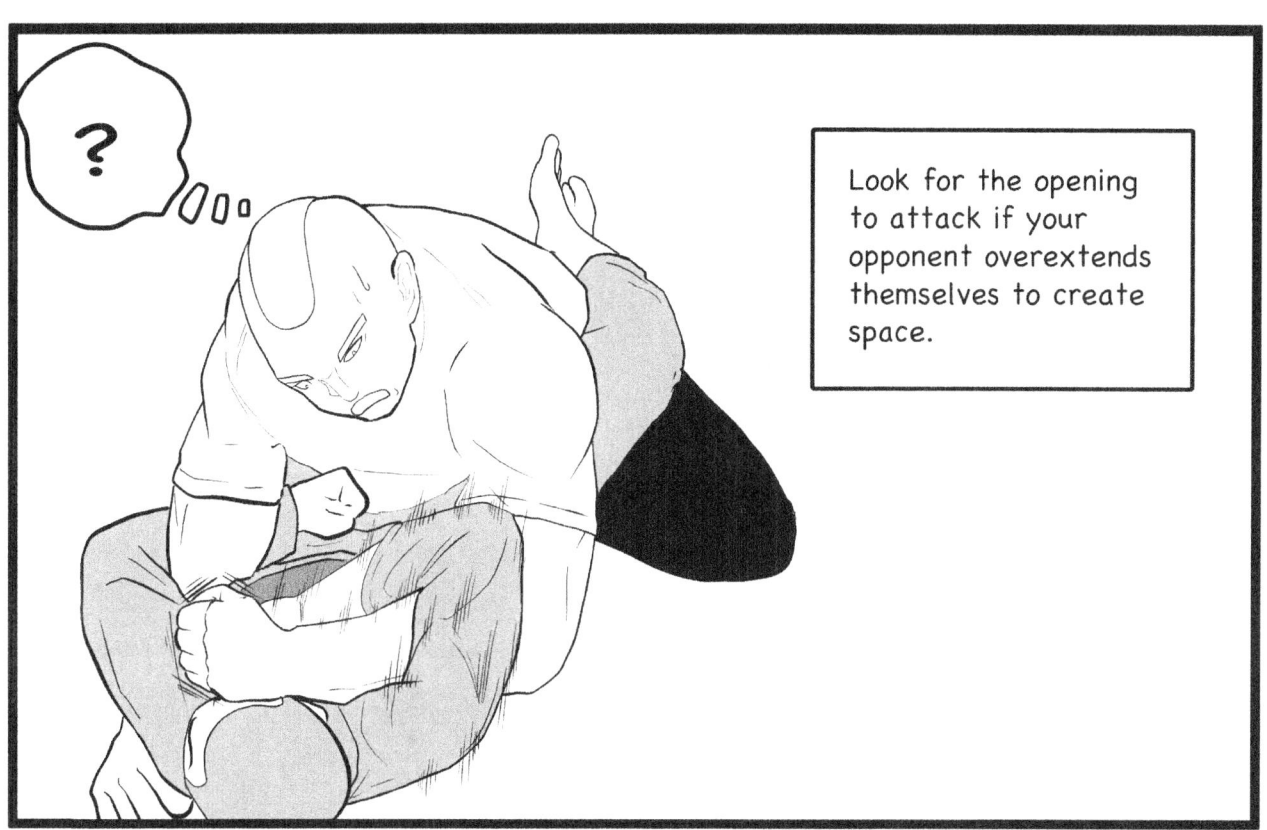

Look for the opening to attack if your opponent overextends themselves to create space.

The attack must be fluid and smooth, with no break between the movements.

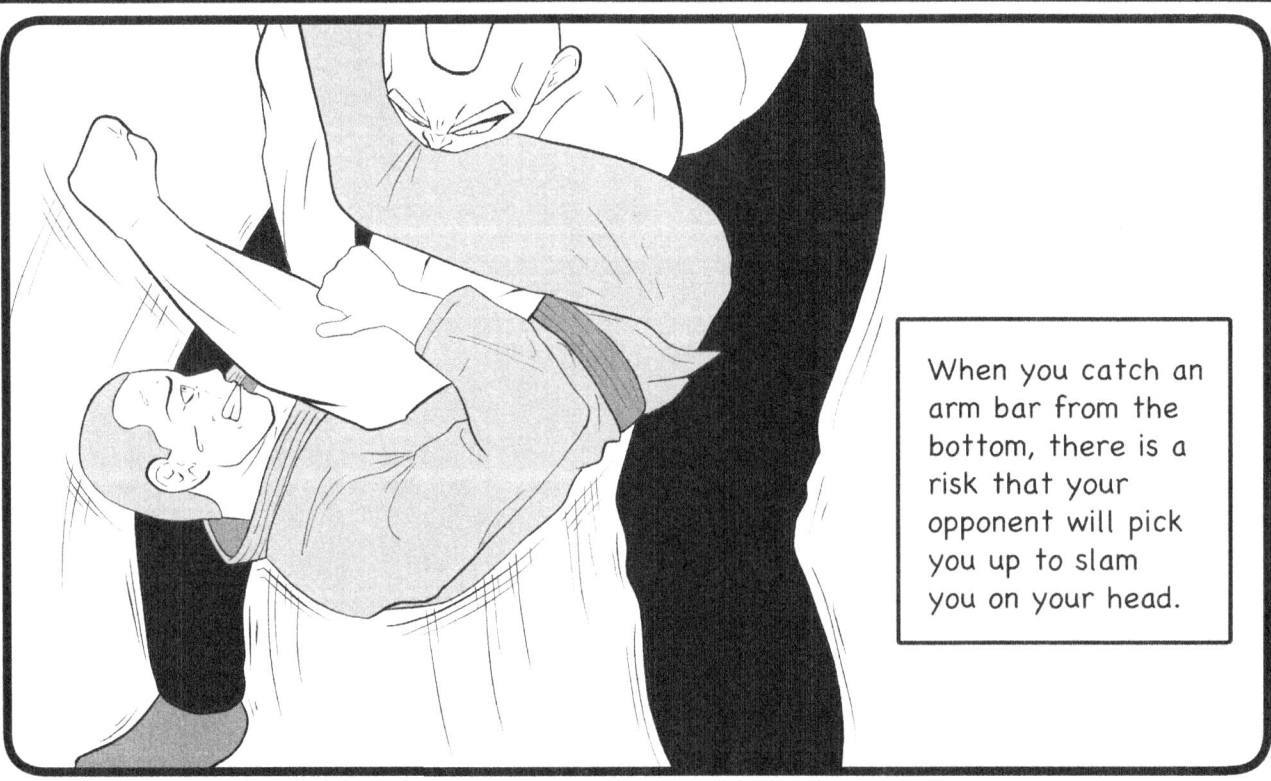

When you catch an arm bar from the bottom, there is a risk that your opponent will pick you up to slam you on your head.

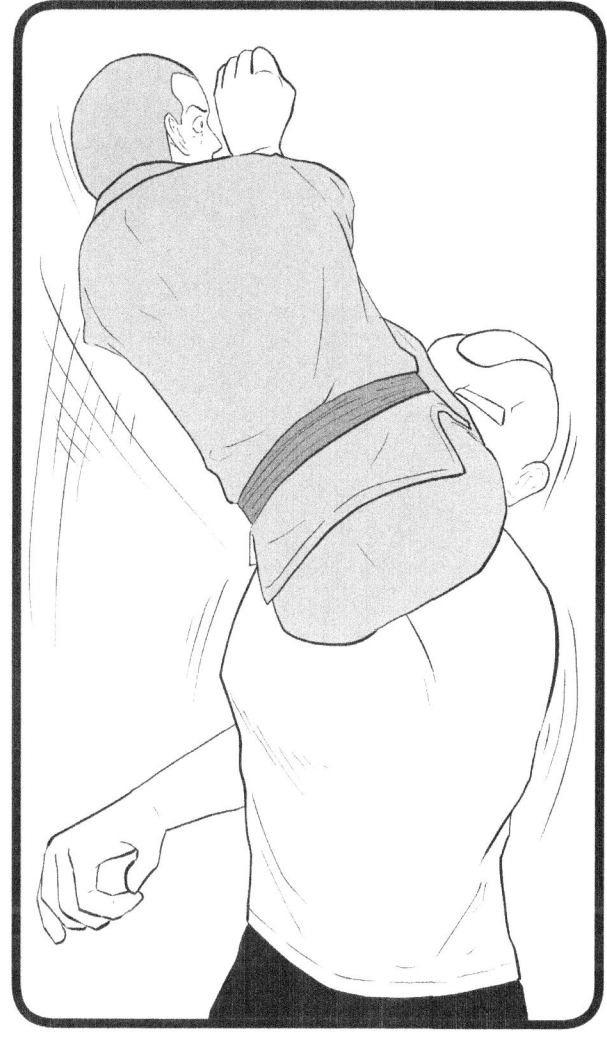

To prevent being picked up by your opponent, hook and pull your opponent's leg to use it as an anchor and pull them off balance.

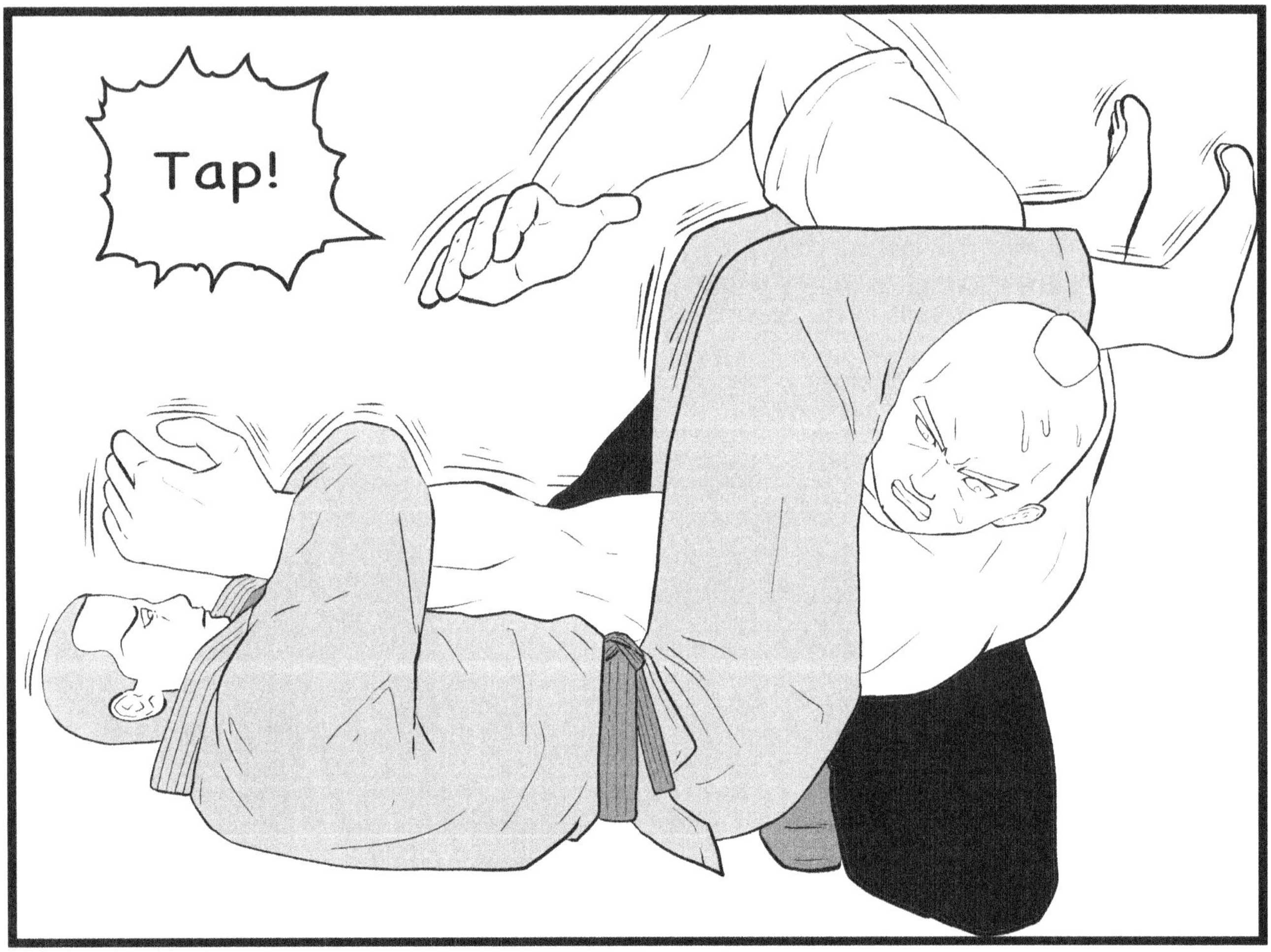

FIGHT TECHNIQUE BREAKDOWN!

In this chapter, you will see instructions for positions where the characters are described doing movements on just one side. The positions can be done on either side but has been illustrated on just one side for simplicity.

FROM THE BOOK !
GUARD BOTTOM ARMBAR

1. Grip your opponent's head with your right hand. Grip your opponents arm with your left hand.

2. Place the ball of your left foot on your opponent's right hip.

3. Push the inside of your left knee into your opponent.

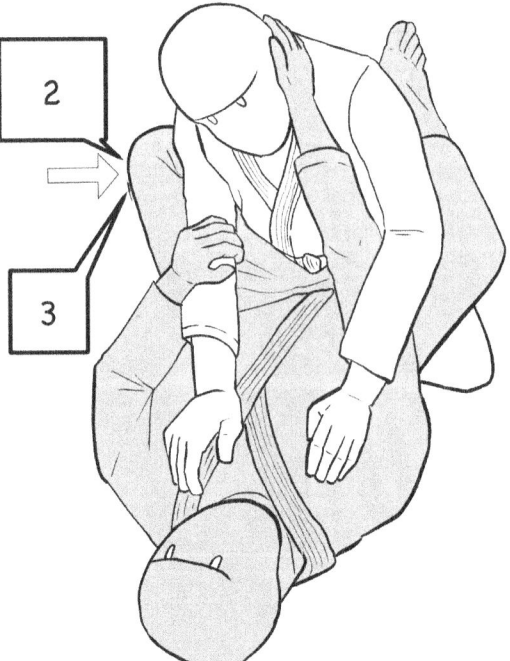

FROM THE BOOK !

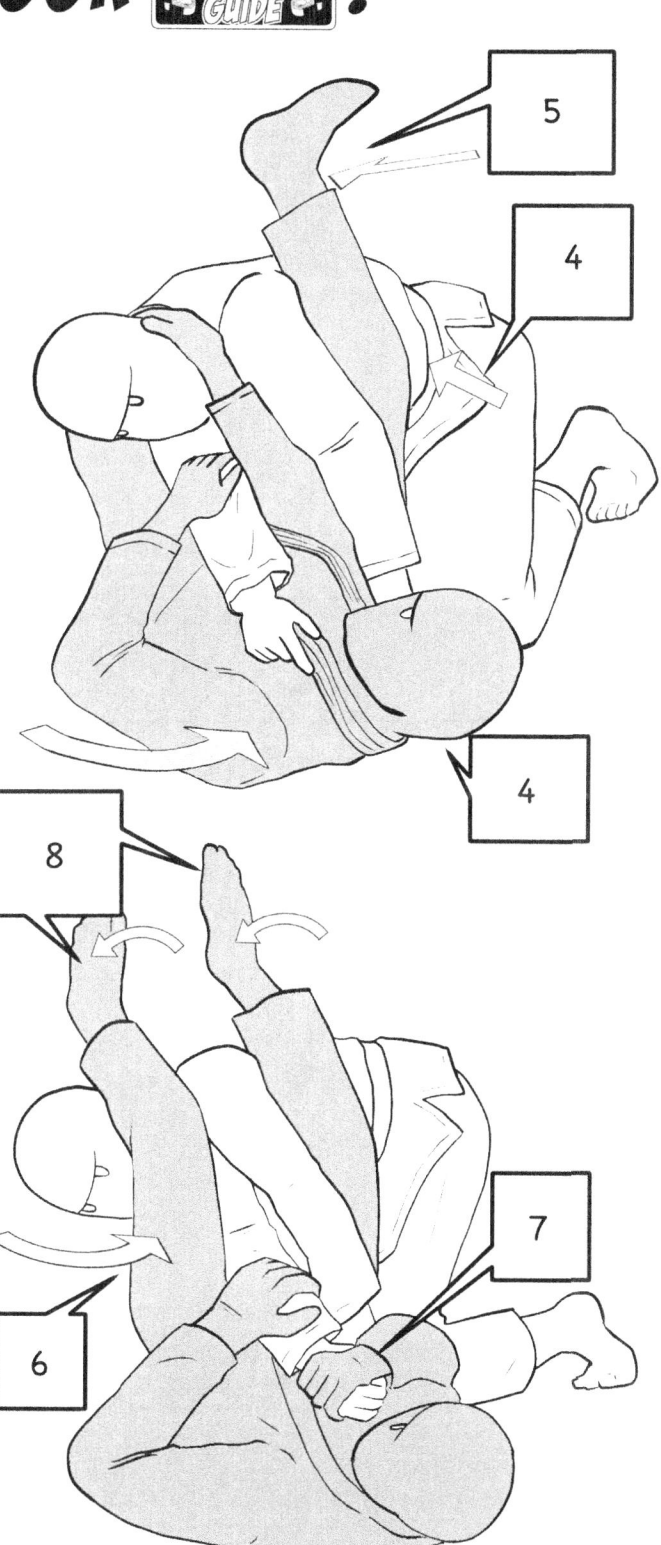

4. Push off of your left foot and swing your right shoulder by your opponent's left knee Simultaneously, swing your right leg deep into your opponent's armpit.

5. Drive your opponent's torso down with your right leg. This will keep your opponent off balance.

6. Swing your left leg over your opponent's head.

7. Release the head with your right hand and grab your opponent's hand and attach it to the middle of your chest. Point your opponent's right thumb up.

8. Drive your heels down, left heel pushing your opponent's head down, right heel pushing your opponent's torso down. Drive your hips up slowly till your opponent's elbow locks out.

THANK YOU FOR READING!

I was first introduced to Jiu Jitsu by my friends in a form of watching old school no holds barred fighting. I was instantly captivated by it. After a few sessions of wrestling my friends in their living room, I knew that I wanted to learn Jiu Jitsu. As I trained Jiu Jitsu and watched more fights, I had a dream of fighting in the cage like my Jiu Jitsu heroes and someday earning my black belt. As a 23 year old in 2001, it seemed like impossible dreams. I'm so grateful that I have gotten to reach these goals and that I now get to teach Jiu Jitsu for a living.

I hope Jiu Jitsu becomes as special a part of your life as it has for me!

Keisuke Andrew

If you liked this book, check out Beginner's Jiu Jitsu Guide!

Printed in Great Britain
by Amazon